I0023076

R.D Garratt

Practical Pig-Keeping

A Manual for Amateurs

R.D Garratt

Practical Pig-Keeping
A Manual for Amateurs

ISBN/EAN: 9783742862907

Manufactured in Europe, USA, Canada, Australia, Japa

Cover: Foto ©Andreas Hilbeck / pixelio.de

Manufactured and distributed by brebook publishing software
(www.brebook.com)

R.D Garratt

Practical Pig-Keeping

PRACTICAL

PIG-KEEPING:

A MANUAL FOR AMATEURS,

BASED ON

PERSONAL EXPERIENCE IN BREEDING, FEEDING, AND FATTENING;

ALSO IN

BUYING AND SELLING PIGS AT MARKET PRICES.

BY

R. D. GARRATT.

SECOND EDITION, REVISED & ENLARGED.

LONDON:
L. UPCOTT GILL, 170, STRAND, W.C.

LONDON
L. UPCOTT GILL, LONDON AND COUNTY PRINTING WORKS,
DRURY LANE, W.C.

PREFACE TO THE SECOND EDITION.

THE First Edition of this book, compiled from notes made for some years previously, was published in 1892, and a short appendix on the method of the Government in stamping out swine fever was added in June, 1894. Respecting the general treatment and management of pigs I do not think any revision is even now necessary, for the testimony from readers of all classes is that it has been of practical use to them. Readers, however, should remember that the prices of both pigs and feeding stuffs fluctuate a good deal in a short time, so that anyone reading figures and prices in the present edition must bear in mind that they are given to show comparative value only. There is no sure profit in any livestock industry. Prices of feeding stuffs may go up whilst anyone is breeding or feeding, and trade may be bad when ready to sell, or the reverse. In keeping pigs, as other animals, the owners have to take the bad times with the good. Not in the case of any other animal do prices go from one extreme to the other as they do in that of pigs.

The latter part of the book, where I refer to diseases and sickness amongst pigs, and especially that relating to swine fever, is re-written. Since the First Edition was published, the "Swine

Fever Bill* has been passed into law, giving the Board of Agriculture the power to make regulations for the purpose of stamping out this dreaded disease. A sum is allowed by the Government to compensate the owners, and for general expenses attached to the same. This Act came into operation on November 1st, 1893. The money already spent, however, has been literally thrown away, as swine fever is now as prevalent as ever, although pig-keepers have been put to serious loss by trade being so seriously handicapped, or even stopped.

Whilst disease exists anywhere there cannot be a free buying and selling of pigs. Till it is cleared out of the country the pig-keeping industry cannot be so profitable, nor be carried on to the extent it should be. As it is most important that practical measures be taken to clear the country quickly, before the trade is half ruined in many parts (as it will be under the present restrictions), I shall give my humble but candid opinion how this can be done most quickly, and with the least expense to pig-keepers. I shall speak as a man of experience, and if by stating absolute facts, and by pointing out past blunders, I offend those in authority, it must be remembered that I do so with the best intentions.

Because I happen to buy and sell pigs I have been represented as having self-interest at heart only. In reply to this I can only say that where I suffer in my business through trade being stopped by unreasonable and quite unnecessary restrictions, thousands of breeders and feeders suffer much more; and if I, as a dealer, should benefit by practical measures being taken, and swine fever exterminated, so would thousands of breeders, feeders, butchers, and consumers, and the country at large, and we should feel inclined to go in for breeding and keeping pigs more largely. If all dealers had bought and sold with the care that I have exercised during the last ten years; if the Government had done their part, and outbreaks had been reported and promptly stamped out; and if a proper system of preventing the smuggling of suspected pigs had been adopted, the country might have been comparatively free from the disease long before now, and trade *in healthy pigs* might still have been carried on safely during the time when the fever was being rooted out.

Considering the immense quantity of pig-meats in proportion to beef, mutton, eggs, poultry, &c., imported, it is of vast importance to England that our great foe, swine fever, and that *greater foe* to this industry, stoppage of trade, be both got rid of, and quickly. I therefore, in this edition, not only give the best advice I can on how to manage pigs profitably, but also enter largely into the means of doing away with the greatest drawback to making them profitable, in the hope that the matter may be looked into by all well-wishers of our English producers, the Government of the day, and our representatives in Parliament.

As stated in the First Edition, I court fair criticism, on this latter subject especially. I should like to hear what other practical men have to suggest, or what amendments they may make to my suggestion. I do not ask for the opinion of *theorists* of no practical experience in pig-keeping. These have done too much mischief in the past, and too much of their theoretical advice has been listened to and acted upon. We want a consensus of opinion from *working* pig-keepers, butchers, &c., whose animals have been condemned. "In the multitude of counsellors" (who know what they are speaking upon) "there is safety."

Explanation of Pig Terms.—Doing business with pig-keepers in all parts, I have in a great measure come to understand the varied local phraseology and terms used amongst pig-keepers, which at one time were very confusing, and a little explanation here may save the reader any misunderstanding.

A *gill*, *yell*, or *hill*, is an unspayed female breeding pig, and is so called until it has left its first litter.

A *barrow hog* is a boar pig, castrated when young for feeding.

A *hog* is a pig for feeding. The term *hog* is also used for a breeding boar.

A *brawn* is a young uncastrated male.

A *stag-hog* or *boar* is a boar that has been used for breeding and castrated.

Litter, or *farrow*, is the whole family a sow suckles at one time.

Teats and *dills* are the same.

Bag and *udder* are identical.

A *stone* of meat, where I mention it, is 8lb.—the London dead meat weight. In some parts the *stone* is 14lb. These must not be confused.

A *score* is 20lb. of carcase meat.

Middlings, *dun*, *sharps*, *toppings*, &c., are the same.

Bran is the outer skin of wheat.

Pollard is the finer and inferior parts of bran.

R. D. GARRATT.

BARTON, NEAR AMPTHILL, BEDS.

PRACTICAL PIG-KEEPING.

Introduction.—In writing a treatise on pigs, let the reader in the first place understand that I am not a pedigree breeder or a pig-fancier, and that this is not written for the benefit of pedigree breeders. I look at pig-breeding from the standpoint of profit derived in selling the pigs at ordinary market prices. I have bred a large number, and have also reared a great many, run them on as stores, and finished many off for the butcher. At times I have had "bad luck," as it is called, and have had "good fortune" at other times; and I have been subject to losses and reverses, as all other breeders and feeders must have been. I have made mistakes in management and committed errors of judgment at times, which every one is liable to; but whether my treatment and method have in the long run been found successful, or otherwise, I am willing to give the reader the benefit of my experience; holding that if a writer tells others where he has failed, he confers quite as much benefit as by telling them where he has succeeded. Nothing teaches a man like experience, but this often has to be dearly bought, and timely advice may save a man from losing many pounds. No one who has in the end succeeded need be ashamed of a few mistakes, but should point them out as a warning to others.

In publishing information on any practical subject like pig-breeding, which is a very important subject, considering the scale on which the breeding, feeding, and fattening of pigs are now conducted in this country, it behoves the writer to be very careful that all statements made are true; that they have been put to the test, and will stand scrutinising; that he has had practical experience of the same, and that it is not mere hearsay or theory, or if so, he should distinctly state the same, and give the reader to understand that it is only brought forward for the consideration of persons engaged in the particular occupation. If quotations are made from any other authorities' writings, then to be honest the writer ought to distinctly state who is the authority he quotes from. A man may be sadly misled by wrong advice, and whether he be a large capitalist or a small man, advice wrongly given may cause great comparative loss.

There are rules which in nineteen out of twenty cases may be relied on. The twentieth may be an exception, but instead of giving an exceptional occurrence as an exceptional one, many writers, because of its novelty, would state it as a common fact, and by so doing might unwittingly mislead a novice into a piece of mismanagement. Any advice I may distinctly give in this work, however, the reader may confidently act on. If it is a quotation from any other writer, I shall state so, and if it is simply as a proposition for the reader to give it a trial in a small way before embarking in it in a general way, then I shall distinctly state it as a theory. Some readers may think that I, being thoroughly acquainted with pig-keeping in all its branches, might have tested any theory myself and have known the result: I can only say that it would have been impracticable as I was situated. What would be practicable on a farm would be impossible in the suburbs of a town, or in any thickly-populated district, and *vice versâ*. What would answer in Yorkshire would not answer perhaps in another part of the country as people must prepare for the demand, and not expect the markets to receive just what they may think well to get ready. A good deal of difference in the final balance-sheet, if a feeder keeps one, would be the result of studying the demand.

Pig-keeping is carried on under very various conditions. Not only is the general farmer interested, but many classes besides. Tell a man he must let his sows out in an orchard, when he has only a stye at the end of the garden, and he would want to know whether it would be wise to keep one as he was situated, and the best way to manage. Of course, he must do the best he can under the circumstances, and a hint of how they have been managed successfully in this way would be welcomed by a man going in for keeping one.

Review of the Trade, Past, Present, and Prospective.—For some time previous to 1889-90, sows, young pigs, and stores were in fair demand, and profitable prices could be obtained for good stuff; but fat hogs sold at middling prices only. About the end of 1890, feeding stuffs advanced in price, and there was a glut of sows, stores, and fat hogs in the markets and sales. Everybody seemed to be a seller, and buyers being few, the animals had to be sacrificed at low prices. In fact trade had not been so bad for many years as it was at this time and during 1891. Many seemed anxious to clear out; and instead of culling out their worst sows, they got rid of nearly or quite all. With the new year (1892) came a change, and, as I anticipated, suddenly there was a short supply of pigs in the country. Up went prices with a bound, and sows and stores doubled their value in very little time. Then for some time those who had kept their best sows on, and who had some really good ones, made some money by breeding. Anything good in breeding and store stock sold well. These good prices induced more people to go in for breeding, so that there came a too large supply, and prices of both fat and store stock have now (Nov., 1896) for the last eighteen months or more been bad; in fact a lot of money has been lost by feeding pigs, and bad prices have been obtained for stores as a consequence. The supply has exceeded the demand The imports of pig-meat from America and the

Continent has also been exceedingly heavy. There have been more pigs, both stores and fat, than buyers. Districts that breed largely, and have a large quantity for export, have, through the restrictions imposed in consequence of swine fever, had the usual channels for customers shut against them. Fat hogs have been sent to the markets and sales, and had to be killed directly, and distant curers have been prevented from buying and moving, so that when all local buyers have had their wants supplied, the surplus animals have been disposed of at a severe loss to the sender. The pigs were there, and the owner has often had to stand by and see them sold at a ruinous price. When butchers are compelled to kill in three days in hot weather, however willing they may be to buy a pound's worth of meat for sixteen shillings, they dare not bid that. All these things combined have caused the serious low prices and loss to those who breed or feed for sale.

Looking into the future, I see a chance of improved prices, if trade be not so seriously handicapped by the restrictions alluded to above. Many are so discouraged through the bad prices and stoppage of sale, that they are giving up in disgust, selling off their best sows, and having what they call "a good clear out." Certainly a lot of good useful breeding sows have been fed and killed lately through the bad prices obtained and stoppage of sale; and, if this goes on, the restrictions are taken off, and some workable measure is adopted by the Government, I anticipate paying prices in the near future. Success, however, greatly depends on the price of feeding-stuffs, and the imports of pig-meat from abroad. One thing I can say—America, with her system of maize feeding, will never produce a good piece of bacon, and good English barley-meal-fed animals will be in request. What Great Britain has to fear are Denmark and other Continental countries that can produce a good piece of bacon if they like, and where pig-keeping and bacon-curing are fostered, instead of hampered, by the respective Governments.

Let pig-keepers, however, keep good stock, not get overdone, and treat the animals well, remembering that six sows well seen after pay better than twelve given only the same attention and time, and the same with feeding pigs. Taking one time with another, I think they can make this industry pay as well as, or better than, any other kind of livestock or farm produce, in spite of the neglect it has received from the Government and County Councils, &c., in comparison with poultry-keeping, bee-keeping, and other smaller rural industries.

The Fraud of Selling Foreign-fed Pig-meats as English.—This is carried on to a large extent, people being wilfully led to believe that what they buy is not foreign; it shows that the consumer generally has a preference for English against foreign meat, and he has good ground for his prejudice, or rather preference. Whilst not trying to put a block before the wheel of free trade, I must protest against this fraud. It is my belief that if it were made impossible to sell foreign pig-meats as English, it would be a great help to our home trade. How is this to be done? It can be effected in two ways: First, the Government should pass a *workable* Act, and, secondly, English producers should combine, as recommended on page 48. That paragraph was written some time ago, and since then Lord Winchilsea has tried to give this practical effect with a good many English products, by starting an association in London to sell English produce only, having buying connections about the country, with an intention of making other provincial branches for selling. This association is in its infancy, having only recently commenced work. Whether it succeeds or not, will depend on two things: First, good practical management, and, secondly, the sympathy and patronage of the public. Both the consumer and the producer have suffered from misrepresentation in the past; but, unless they make up their minds to give the association a fair trial, it will not succeed. I would also ask my readers not to complain if prices received seem low to the producer, or those paid comparatively high to the consumer, at first: these will be adjusted in time. It would be a fine thing for the producer to get a steady, reliable market for his pork and bacon, instead of having to face the fluctuations in prices, which are often ruinous. To the consumer it would be a good thing to get really first-class barley-meal and pea-fed pork and bacon at a fair price, instead of often paying the same price for cheap maize-fed and inferior pork and bacon, that wastes in cooking, and is bad eating into the bargain. I am not asked to puff this concern, and have no interest whatever in it. I only mention it through a wish that it may prove a help to the pig-keeping industry in England. Anyone having genuine English produce to sell, or buyers who prefer English to foreign eggs, butter, pork, bacon, and other produce, should communicate with The Secretary, the British Produce Supply Association, Winchilsea House, Long Acre, London.

Do Pigs Pay?—It is asserted by some writers that pigs do not pay if all the food has to be bought, and that the only way they can be made profitable is as consumers of waste products, when what would otherwise be useless is converted into pork, and eventually into hard cash. But this is only because they have been told so, and it has in course of time become a common saying, that is set down as a hard-and-fast rule. That pigs can be made to pay for their breeding, feeding, and fattening, even with purchasing all the food, I can vouch for from experience; but only by good management will they be made profitable.

Bad Luck and Reverses in Pig-keeping.—With the best management, study, and attention, there will be at times losses and reverses; and a run of bad luck may make anyone down-hearted, and at times make the most persevering inclined to "throw up the sponge." I have been in this position, and have had my bad times. I had them when quite a boy, when I was allowed to keep a few sows and feeding-pigs on the farm. On one occasion two or three sows came down with the milk fever about the same time, sows that with a good litter a week old would have been worth £6 or more each, and was afraid of losing the lot; being very thankful to keep the sows alive and get off with the loss of the pigs. Then when I thought I had got a little straight, I had sows farrow with only an average of three or four each. I have had a sow farrow unawares on a cold night, and a good litter get nearly all perished; a sow set to and kill her progeny; and a sow due to farrow in about a month, without any warning suddenly come in season, and instead of being worth £4 or £5, turn out to be worth 60s. I have had a lot of heavy pigs suddenly set on to one of their fellows, and the next time I fed them found it dead, and nipped nearly to pieces. I have lost pigs through colds, husks, and the innumerable complaints pigs are liable to; and had good litters of pigs which ought to have been worth 20s. get the cramp, and then could not sell them at any price. I have had my fat pigs ready to come out when trade was bad and prices low. More than once have I sat up with a sow all night long, expecting her to farrow before morning—perhaps she was an extra good sort, bought at a high price, and looked promising and like having a fine litter of pigs—but, after being nearly perished with cold, have sometimes by morning been rewarded with *two pigs.*

These things are all discouraging, and enough to make anyone shy of going into pig-keeping, if I were to leave off here. But my motive in making these statements is rather as an encouragement to those that may be in a small or larger way of pig-keeping, and having experienced any of these losses, have become down-hearted because of them. Let them remember that others have been placed in the same position. Some of the most persevering, and in the long run successful, men have passed through the same. Some of these losses will occur with the oldest and most experienced men, and with the wisest treatment. But I have had *losses that might have been prevented*, or *at least lessened*, if I had acted differently to what I did at the time, and had been more experienced.

A Little Plain Advice to Novices.—Another thing I hope to do in describing some of the risks pig-keepers have to run, is *to do away with the idea many people have that pig-keeping is all profit.* The idea is strongly in the minds of some people, mostly town clerks, and others engaged in business in large towns, who have to work hard for a living in their vocation. They have an idea that to have a small place in the country, a small holding, and a few acres of ground, and to go in for poultry-farming and pig-keeping, and perhaps a cow, would be a fine thing. They say that eggs being very dear, poultry must be profitable altogether; and that the pigs will make a good return; and altogether such a beautiful picture of the imagination is drawn, that it seems a pity to do away with the illusion. I have heard the tale from the lips of city friends, and have silently let them believe it. But if I knew they seriously contemplated trying it, of course I would warn them of the results.

There is no doubt many a townsman who occasionally has a holiday in the country, who will glean a little here and a little there, and being a fluent and convincing writer, would make one believe almost against his better judgment. Some writers to this day assert that a living may be got out of a poultry-farm, pure and simple, in which the eggs are worth market price for eating on the farm only, and the fowls sold at an ordinary price each for killing, and that a good income may be made in this way; but I have never known it done yet. I mention this to warn any inexperienced person not to be led away by the illusion. Enthusiasm is very well for spurring on a man in the right course, but there is something more than this wanted to make a man successful. The most enthusiastic at the beginning are often the least likely to stand a rebuff.

Successful pig-keeping requires the steady, hard-headed plodder, who, when he has losses, makes his loss as little as he can; who, if he sees himself in a position where he is liable to lose £10, works hard to lose only £5; or if he cannot quite save £5 from being lost, he will not lose any more than he can help; who, if he has lost anything through unwitting mismanagement or error, confesses to himself that he was in error, and makes it a warning to himself in the future; who does not give a thing up as a bad job because of reverses, discouraging and bad as they are at the time, especially if he is a poor man to whom a pound loss or gain is a consideration.

In spite of the risk of losses, I again say that pigs can be made to pay, buying all the food at market price, by careful management, forethought, and attention. "What is worth doing, is worth doing well" is applicable here; or the quotation might be inverted, "What is not worth doing well, is not worth doing at all." Half doing things has been the ruination of many otherwise clever men. Half farming, for instance, has been, and will be, the ruination of many a man. Doing things in a way causing the least trouble is the way with many people who are termed unfortunate when such work makes them pinch.

"If I want anything done properly," many employers of labour say, "I must do it myself," and there is no doubt but that this is the way in pig-keeping; for there is no one, be he ever such a faithful servant, who will give such minute attention as the owner himself. He sees seemingly trifling things that would escape a paid man's notice—things that, however trivial to a superficial observer, are seen by the owner to be of the utmost importance. I do not wish to go into any detailed instances, but such is the case.

Take a cotter with one or two pigs. Who can get them along so fast as he can? They are his own, and he knows that if he gets so much per head out of them, or loses so much, it means so much difference to his pocket. A man who looks at them like that, see how careful he is. The pig is petted and rubbed, and is left by the owner when he has licked and cleaned out his trough and laid down with a grunt of contentment. Should its ordinary feed be put in, and it does not seem to eat much, he will soon find out whether the pig is wrong, or the food, or what is the cause.

A stockman on a farm, or a man having the care of any live animals, who has really at heart their well-being and ultimate profit to their owner, is a boon to his master, and should be treated accordingly, and valued at his true worth: and there ought to be a mutual understanding between master and servant, that what is one's interest should be the other's; and a few shillings a week is a trifle out of the master's pocket for such a man as this, contrasted with a dilatory, thick-headed, selfish man, who is afraid that he does not have his full meal-time, or that he cannot get away at night in good time.

Take, for instance, a shepherd, or a horse-keeper, or anyone who has live stock under his care: not only will an interested man work for his master when on the farm, but he will make a study of the well-doing of what he has under his care when he is away. "They are few and far between," some may say. Then let those who have them use them well and pay them well.

Pigs as Waste-consumers.—I have stated that pigs can be made to pay, even when all their food has to be purchased; but as consumers of waste they are a *necessity*. In the first place, we will take the waste matter on the farm—offal and damaged corn. On many farms pigs are purchased as a necessity, to eat the stuff out of the way. But a real business man, unless he has other occupation that does not allow him time, ought to make a rough estimate of the difference in various lots of hogs fed, and the different ways they are fed, so that he may know the best way to go to work from time to time to feed his stuff off, and what admixture of offals are best to use. There is also the loose corn lying about during threshing-time, stubbling, and in certain districts the fall of acorns. On the gardening lands there are the offal and otherwise useless potatoes; on the dairy farm, there is the milk to be converted into pork; while with the cotter there are the garden refuse and odds-and-ends to give to the pig. In the large towns, also, there must be a considerable amount of waste matter that no doubt would pay well for collecting and using up, with other foods, as pig-feed.

In obtaining—whether by breeding or purchase—pigs to consume these various waste matters, there is to be considered the sort of pig most suitable for the purpose. And among the most important considerations for the feeder, are the breed of pig, the size and age to eat up the different foods, and lastly, but not of least importance, the outlet for the animals when such matters are consumed, and whether they will pay best as small porkers, or large bacon hogs, or what. The demand in the localities in which they are situated must be the principal guide in this matter.

Piggeries.—I will speak of these under a general head in the first place. A man may be situated in a place where he has various buildings that have not been expressly built for piggeries, and is using them for the purpose. It would be folly to tell him that he had better pull them down and build regular styes of certain dimensions and make. He must use them as he thinks best for the comfort of his stock. On a farm there are certain buildings that during some part of the year, when the stock is out to grass, are more suitable than the regular styes—large open hovels, for instance, for stores or fattening hogs, or, if properly partitioned off, for sows and pigs.

Build on High Ground.—In putting up piggeries, or using any buildings for that purpose, the first thing, and really the fundamental one, is to have the floor of the styes on a high, dry position. It is a necessity for the well-being of the stock that the piggery stands on high ground. It should be, if possible, on a natural rise, so that the water can run away both before and behind, and none can lodge in the styes. If the bottom lies low and damp, pigs will never thrive during seven or eight months of the year at least, and if the bottom is damp, they will not do well at any time. If the styes are built on the level ground, they should be well raised with chalk or earth, so that no water can enter or stand round the outside.

The bottom of the styes should be made of chalk or hurlock, rammed down hard. Bricks I do not like, as I find pigs do not do well on them. Boards are dry, and would suit pigs well, but they are not more generally used because they absorb and retain the moisture, and harbour disease and bad smells. The foundations, and for a certain height, are, no doubt, best bricked, as having strength and being more lasting than wood. The rest of the outside should be of stout boards, and it is a good plan to have a board to raise or shut, to let in more or less air, according to the weather.

A pig requires to be kept warm and free from draughts, and yet have plenty of air and ventilation. The piggeries should therefore be built with a *good high roof*, and if in a range the top should be open, so that the air can draw right along. Low, stuffy styes are neither healthy nor wholesome for pigs, and they will not do so well as they would in high and airy ones. If the styes are built very low, the wind will blow directly on the pigs when air is let in, which should be avoided. Therefore, the large pig-keeper, or the small cotter, in putting up new styes, in the first place should see that they are built on good high ground, and are lofty and spacious, for by this means they can be made both healthy and comfortable.

The best roof, no doubt, is thatch, as although this may be more trouble in putting on and keeping in repair, pigs will do better under it than under anything else. Tiles are tidy, and I should prefer them for a piggery on a large scale. Slates or galvanised iron or zinc roofing I should not use on any account, as both (especially the latter) are so very hot in the summer's sun that pigs could not be under them with any comfort; while in wet weather zinc roofing is very cold, and the damp is sure to get through.

For the winter months of the year there is no doubt that closed-in styes are best, that is if they are spacious and airy, as recommended. When the weather is wet and cold, and pigs come outside to feed, they get cold and shivering, and by treading about the wet straw and then on the bedding, they make this wet and damp. Still, I should, in putting up any building, always make it with a small yard attached, so that the animals can be fed inside or out, according to what they are, and the time of the year. By having a door as well, the feeder can shut them in altogether or not, as he thinks well; and if the buildings are well laid, troughed, and built on high ground, so that no water can stand in the outside yard, they can lie inside a good roomy place comfortable, dry, and warm.

A good many piggeries are built now completely bricked-in, with a partition up the middle of a range of buildings for the feeder to walk up, with the styes on each side. Such as these I should prefer to see bricked-up about a yard high, and the rest boarded, and also some yards made outside of each place, so that the pigs could get out in the air in the summer weather. Such places as these are very well in the winter for fatting pigs only, but young growing pigs, or sows suckling pigs, require more room and more air during the hot weather. Indeed, it is a mistake altogether to keep sows and pigs, young growing pigs, and store pigs shut up in too close quarters. If they had more freedom and exercise than many do now, they would get on much better. During the summer-time a pig only wants sufficient shelter to keep it from lying in the wet and sun. I have kept them in regular bricked piggeries in a yard, and have knocked up temporary places out in the open, or at the side of a straw-stack, with a few hurdles, just so that the wet did not get in; and being on fresh ground, and with plenty of air, they have done much better than in the best built styes.

Pig-yards on Large Farms.—On all farms where breeding on a large scale is gone in for, a pig-yard should be made quite separate from where other stock and cattle are kept. This, with some neat styes for the breeding-sows, and some other places for store and running pigs, and a good open shed or two for the in-pig sows or larger stores, should be provided. It should be made as large as possible, provided it is well sheltered from the cold winds. If some large open hovels or sheds are put up, they should have their backs towards the cold quarters, and they will then only catch the warmer winds, and will also shelter the other styes. Where the breeding and feeding are carried on on a smaller scale, the owner must adapt himself to his circumstances, and make the best use of the places he has; and a little alteration in sheltering a rather bleak place, or making a too close place a little more airy, can always be made by a man who has the energy and thoughtfulness to do it. This may generally be said of the cotter or man who only keeps a few pigs or a sow, as he will quickly see how things are.

In addition to seeing that the pigs lie high and dry, a regular pig-yard, or where the pigs are kept, should also be well provided with a good outlet for water, either a slant being made so that any water that falls in the yard can quickly drain away, or a drain from a certain point in the yard where the water soaks should be provided, so that none can stand about. If the buildings are well eave-troughed all round, and care be taken to clean them out and keep them clear, there will not be a sloppy place for the pigs to run about, and they will do much better than if running up to their bellies in mud and dung.

I have described the yards and buildings from a general point of view, and think it will be best to give particulars of breeding-styes at the time I am treating on the management of breeding-sows, &c.

Profitable and Unprofitable Kinds of Pigs.—A man without experience intending to go in for breeding or keeping pigs would naturally in the first place inquire, "What is the *best and most profitable sort* of pigs to keep?" If he inquired of one who had made a study of and kept a *good sort of white pigs*, he would be informed that there was none to come up to *white pigs* to keep. If he inquired of a *Berkshire* fancier, he would hear that the *Berkshire breed* was the best; of a *Tamworth* fancier, and he would be advised to go in for the *Tamworth breed.* But there is always allowance to be made for the prejudice of an ardent breeder of any one particular stock against any other breed which he has not studied and become familiar with

Now the breeds of pigs to go in for are those that will make the *most weight* of *best quality* meat in *least time*, and at *lowest cost*. There are pigs called White Yorkshires, Black Berkshires, and Tamworths, that are so in name, but are useless for profit. There are also others of these breeds that the owners would quickly pit against any breed that could be named. In short, there are good-paying pigs of all breeds, and there are others that should never have been bred. One sound rule to go by in buying, is to go in for good heavy pigs when they are ready to come away from the sow. Such pigs as these are bound to pay for keeping. In selecting a breed of pigs, the buyer must ask himself in the first place, what he intends to do with them when he has them for sale. Suppose he intends breeding them, and selling off from the sow; or running on for stores, and then selling; or purchasing, running through the summer, and making into large bacon hogs; or only making small porkers; then he must get the sorts he wants to make the best of.

The White Yorkshire Breed.—In Yorkshire, and that part of the country, where pigs are made into extra large bacon hogs, the large white pigs are kept or purchased; and a large-framed growing white pig, with plenty of timber underneath, also fine-haired and thin-skinned, is the sort preferred. There is no one who knows what a good pig is better than a Yorkshireman. In purchasing for running on, he will not have a small runty pig at a gift; whilst for a best quality large-growing pig, as described above, he is always willing to give a fair price; and he is wise in this matter, as they are really the cheapest. Therefore, if the reader is going in for breeding pigs to make into large bacon hogs, or to purchase for feeding into bacon, nothing will come before the large white breed. This breed should be square made, with good wide back and loins, and short-headed. Not necessarily a too bulldog-shaped snout, but not long. It should also have good-sized, upright ears, a good width between them, and bold open eyes. The hair, no doubt, to get good quality, should be thin, some breeders preferring them almost devoid of any, but I like to see them with some long pliable hair, though not thick and bristly. These pigs will often be slightly spotted, this being considered by some feeders a mark of good breeding. Amongst this breed there will be occasionally turned out some of a slightly grey or blue colour. There is a bad sort of pig to be seen of this colour, and also a good sort. See that they are from good growing stock, with good heads and loins, and they will turn out good stock.

The Berkshire Breed, which in its purity should possess white feet, a white star on the forehead, and white on the tip of the tail, is an excellent breed of pig for crossing with the white. It is hardy, and the sows are usually the best of sucklers, although often very savage when with the young. They will also mature very quickly, and be ready for killing at any weight. The meat is also of good quality, and it is a pig that weighs well. There are different classes of the sows kept, some being good large-framed ones, and some more neat and compact. It is kept in its purity in some parts of the country, but strange to say the prejudice against a white pig is so strong in other parts that a white one would not be purchased there on any account. In the county of Somersetshire and also in parts of Gloucestershire, this seems to be the case, and I have been told by buyers from that part that the butchers have such an objection to white pigs that it is useless to fatten them.

I once had an inquiry for four strong heavy stores of the Berkshire breed, and having four just the pick from a lot with a little cross, so that one was completely white, the buyer objected to this one, and could not be prevailed upon to take it. At another place I recommended a buyer to try some of our best crossed whites, and prevailed on him to take some of them. After he had had them long enough to see how they went on, he wrote me that he found them to do first-class; "but," said he, "the prejudice against any white pigs here is so great, that my recommendation of this breed does not stand for much, I only being an amateur. But I have had some friends in to see them this evening who have hitherto been prejudiced against white ones, and they could not but acknowledge that they are doing quite as well, if not better, than our black breed." Why this prejudice should exist I do not know, but if people want a pig to grow and get to a good weight in good time, I recommend a good white or crossed white.

The Tamworth of the best breed is a good useful pig to cross with the Yorkshire and Berkshire. Hardy, and of best quality meat, it is a sort that will no doubt work its way to the front. I have had first-class pigs from a cross between this and the white breed. They are usually good feeders and doers, and by getting some of the blood amongst our whites, both from high-class stock, some good pigs can always be got. There is a very bad sort of Tamworth breed that may occasionally be seen in the local markets, small, wiry, sharp, long-headed ones, about as big as good-sized rats; and while one lot of first-class growing pigs may be seen here and there, the number of worthless ones will be considerably greater. These, no doubt, cause a prejudice against the whole breed in many parts.

The Tamworth is a good breed, then, to cross, if the best stock are got; and as it is not well known in many parts, and is a breed I am not so fully acquainted with as the two first-mentioned ones, I must recommend it to breeders who at present do not know much of it, to try it, and give it fair play. If this is done, select stock from a reliable source, not pick up a bad specimen, and then condemn the whole breed because of it.

Crossing.—My favourite cross—and I think it cannot be beaten for general purposes—is a good crossed sow put to a good white boar. The Berkshire sows are generally good milkers, but put to the same sort of boar their pigs have not growth enough in the first three or four months for me; but when a regular good Berkshire sow is put to a good white boar, they produce a much quicker growing pig, that will generally do well, and which is almost invariably white. But it is not necessary that sows should be pure bred, it is the boar.

Obtaining blood of high-class boars by crossing, as described, will prevent the breed from deteriorating into mongrels, and will bring the pigs healthy, and as a rule, in good litters. Where pigs are bred in and in too much, even if fresh blood of the same breed be imported, they will not bring such large litters and sizable growing pigs. On most of the farms in Bedfordshire it is a rule to keep a good bred, well-selected boar, and where this is done the pigs are usually kept up to a high standard. There are many small mongrel boars about, and also breeding-sows, which the owners might well know cannot bring good saleable or growing pigs, and it is a sad pity they cannot see their folly in breeding from them. With some men a sow is a sow, but far better had anyone give 70s. for a good sow from a good litter of valuable pigs than buy a bad one for 50s. He should bear in mind that not only has he to make a profit or loss out of the pigs she brings, but there is also *selling day* with the *sow herself*, and a good one will always be worth the extra money given.

Breeds to Avoid.—I think the three breeds mentioned, if used and crossed judiciously, will hold their own against any English breed in the country. And now a few words on some bad breeds. There is a narrow-nosed white pig, with back that corresponds with the nose in being sharp and narrow. It stands high on the legs, and has really no make at all about it. It will feed well, being hardy and hungry, but will eat as much to put on one stone of meat as a good short-headed square pig will to put on double that quantity. It will seemingly do well, and make up a good pig, but runs to leg and belly, and when killed and put on the scales will turn out very deceitful, and take anyone in. Corresponding with this pig is a long, narrow, ugly-sheeted hog, often having large lap ears, but otherwise answering the same description as the former. Another sort is a long, bad-made grey or blue pig. This must not be confused with a grey or blue pig which our best whites often throw, as there is a vast difference in the sorts. There are a large number of these long, narrow pigs bred in different districts, and it is surprising that some good selected stock is not made to replace them. In a great measure carelessness and inattention are to blame, and till pigs are looked at as an important part of the breeder's live stock, from which a profit is to be made, and not merely as scavengers, these bad pigs will be bred.

On *some farms a good sort of sows are kept, of no particular breed*, but good ones for pigs—sows that bring some good heavy pigs at weaning time, and pigs that are known to do well when they are taken away—consequently there is always a ready sale for them at a good fair price, the buyers being well aware that they will pay best. This breed is kept up to a good standard by judicious crossing. If the owner were asked the sort, he would perhaps inform you that the original sow from which they all came was of so-and-so sort and came from so-and-so; which will show you what one good stock sow can do. This is often the case with a man who keeps only one or two sows. He can always dispose of his pigs at a good price, and get a name for bringing good stock, his pigs, by extra inquiry for them, making an extra long price. Yet on being told so, he will inform you that he sells his pigs the cheapest in the village. And this is really the case, for although the price is high according to the age, they are pigs that will make into porkers before some start to grow, and for every 1s. laid out will show a good return. Twenty shillings each for pigs about nine or ten weeks old seems a long price, but they are the cheapest pigs to buy, the most profitable to breed, and the pigs that pay to keep on and fatten.

Yes, these are the pigs that pay to keep. Never mind whether they are white, black, mixed, or any other sort. Such pigs as these are not narrow-faced, narrow-backed pigs. They are good, fairly short-headed, square, broad-backed, well-made pigs. I would advise you to go and select some gilts out of a litter of about ten such as described above, and a boar to match, and you will get a breed that no pedigree breeder in the country can beat, if he charges you 42s. at weaning-time.

Before leaving this part of the subject, we have the consumer to study. People do not like either pork or bacon too fat. I think a bacon-curer will tell you that to get high-class meat you must breed good lengthy pigs, and not the small rolly-poly sort, that are all fat. I think a good lengthy white breed, not too bony and rompy, nor too small and compact, turns out good meat, which may be further improved in the grain by crossing either with a Berkshire of the larger sorts or with a Tamworth.

The Use of Pedigree Stock.—In recommending good crosses, I am not under-valuing pedigree herds when kept in their right place. Any live stock would deteriorate into mongrels if high-class blood was not mixed with them, and pure-bred animals on the male side are required amongst any sows to keep them up to a good standard. But any man who keeps a pedigree herd of pigs on purpose to raise pigs for feeding, will find it does not answer as well as judicious crossing—by keeping a good pure-bred boar and judiciously crossing him with his stock sows. Even when doing this, I would rather buy a pure-bred boar from good well-known stock, than buy one direct from a pedigree herd; my reason being that, as a rule, our pedigree herds are too artificially reared and fed. In getting up for show and selling purposes, all manner of expedients are used (cost often not being brought into account) to get the animals in high condition for showing. They are fed on warm and seasoned foods, and fussed and messed up so that when they go into a farmer's yard and are fed in the ordinary way, they for a time go back; while if there is much work to do, they will get off their feed and be dainty; and when this is the case, it must have a bad effect on the future litters.

In *selecting a boar* it would no doubt be best to pick one from a litter before weaning, and it should be from a good fair litter in number, and sizable. If the litter is uneven, I would discard it, for I would rather have a *small boar, if well-made and out of a fairly even litter*, than an extra-sized one, the pick of an uneven litter.

Before I finish with the breed and sorts of pigs, I repeat my advice to intending breeders, as it has such an important effect on the profit and loss—*Go in for good stock; Select good gilts from reliable stock;* see the litter yourself if you can; see how many the sow has; find out what breed they came from. If you buy a sow, do not be led away by the look of one because she is handsome and a pretty picture. Ascertain what stock she came from, and if she has brought any pigs up, and how. If you can do so, buy a sow off of her pigs and from a good lot; and if she be poor and pulled down in condition do not despise her because of that. Buy her on the merit of the pigs she has brought. I do not like sows that suckle *too free*, so as to get pulled down too weak; I would rather have one that brings a good litter of pigs, and keeps a little meat on herself. But if a sow can bring a good lot of pigs, buy her, even if you have to give over ordinary market price. In buying a young boar, it is unwise to be niggardly over a few shillings, when you consider the importance in making an estimate of the number of pigs you are likely to breed. The *importance of keeping good stock* is evident when you consider that you will have just the same work and trouble with inferior ones as with good ones. You will require just the same room and be at quite as much expense with bad as with good ones. Furthermore, you can always sell your surplus stock at a fair price, winter and summer; whilst if they are bad sorts, you will have a good deal of trouble to dispose of them, even at a very low price. If you keep good ones on, you can make them pay; and good growing young pigs in the middle of winter will pay you money, whereas bad sorts will only be a source of trouble.

To those purchasing pigs for feeding, the watchword should be "good sorts at a fair price" rather than "bad sorts very cheap." Do not stick out for a few shillings on a good litter; for if they seem rather dear, they are much cheaper than small, low-priced ones. During the summer months, when there is a trade for pigs off the sow, they can often be bought at 10s. or under, and the owner only too glad to get them off his hands; whilst many good strong litters are making 15s. to 18s. and upwards, and even then the low-priced ones are dear and the 18s. ones cheap. At the time of correcting this, however, pigs are worth but little more than half these prices. When you consider that one lot will grow and make some great hogs in half the time that it takes others, it must stand to reason that the good ones are the most profitable. Where a breeder does well and gets money by a sow, then those pigs, if sold, with proper treatment will go and pay well. On the other hand, where a breeder after selling small pigs without any growth in them at a low price, and puts nothing in his pocket, then I know the feeder will see no return besides cost for a considerable time.

Breeding.—No one should go in for breeding pigs unless he has ample room and convenience for that purpose, and is also in a position to give full and regular attention, either personally or otherwise. Anyone can keep a pig, or a few pigs, and feed them on in a place roughly but comfortably made for that purpose. There must be not only sufficient room in the stye to keep a sow and pigs, but there must be outdoor accommodation in the shape of an orchard or meadow. It is as necessary for the young growing pig and the sow that they should have a run and plenty of exercise as it is that they should have housing and food.

Many cotters or small tradesmen keep a sow for breeding without a meadow or run for the pigs on the grounds, but the successful ones may be seen in the summer evenings watching them out for a run down the grass sides of the road; or the wife, if she is a general manager, may sometimes be seen, with plait in hand, watching them out for a run. It is as natural now for young growing pigs to get out like this and dig and root and eat some earthy matter as it was when they were in a wild state. If the young sucking pig cannot be let out and have its run, care must be taken that it has plenty of green food, cinders, and earth, and whatever it would get at if let out; and even then the exercise will be missed, for it is next to impossible to bring up a growing healthy lot of pigs shut up in a cramped place. I do not say that they are not bred successfully in good roomy places, but many ills are caused by this way of breeding them. They will often go humpbacked, get crampy, scour, and do badly, all of which might in a great measure be avoided by plenty of outdoor exercise. No breeder, then, is in a good position for breeding unless he has an orchard or a run out of the stye somewhere.

Pig breeders may be divided into two classes—the *farmer*, who may keep from three or four sows up to twenty or more; and the *tradesman*, or *labourer*, who keeps one, two, or more. In the case of the farmer, he usually has his range of styes or pig-yard, and the attention and care are left to the stock-man, perhaps assisted by the owner. In the latter case there is a regular routine as regards feeding, the mode of pigging the sows, and general treatment.

The tradesman or cotter generally tends himself or by irregular help. He may have places built on purpose or put up some himself; and, as I mentioned under "General Housing," the latter are often the more suitable. Regular farm styes may be costly but quite unsuitable.

Suppose a man was entering on a farm, on which there was a good range of regularly built styes, but too close and bricked in, he would certainly not want to pull them down, so he must alter and make them comfortable. If they are bricked in all round, he can easily let some air in over the top by taking out some of the bricks; and the same with the yard outside, he must use his judgment in the matter.

Selecting Gilts for Breeding.—In describing the different breeds of pigs, I mentioned that it would be best either to select some gilts out of a litter before they were taken from the sow, and the same with the boar, or obtain reliable sows when their pigs are ready to wean from them. In doing the former, it should in the first place be ascertained that each gilt has twelve good regular teats or dills, and that none of these are blind or false. If it has fourteen dills, it will be better. Those that have the dills well forward should be selected, as a good sow ought not to have them too far back, or the hind ones will contain but little milk. It is not always the largest of the litter that turn out the best breeding sows, and I should not advise anyone to pick out the largest except it has special recommendation in being well dilled.

It is a curious, and not generally known fact, that if you pick out one of the largest gilts and an extra small one from a good litter, that the latter will often turn out the best breeder; will bring the largest number of pigs in a litter, and suckle them the best. Strange as this seems, I have proved it myself, and have seen many instances of it over again. But I hope no intending breeder will misunderstand me, and pick out a stunted gilt from a lot of pigs he knows nothing about. Have them from a good sow, one that has proved a good mother in bringing a good valuable litter up, and that has been got by a good boar. Suppose this sow has ten or twelve good pigs, with the exception of one, that is undersized but well made and has fourteen good dills, that one is as likely to turn out the best mother as not; but I would advise the selection of those with the most numerous and regular teats, irrespective of size, but not to select the least except they are teated better than the larger ones.

Gilts picked out for breeding would no doubt be best of a summer's litter for growth. But as most breeders like to have the two litters come, to make the best average prices they must be selected for this purpose. January and July are the best months of the year to get sows to come down, and there is no doubt but that a good time to get the gilt to pig the first time is in July. To get it to do this it should be from a sow that pigs about that time, and would be weaned, say, the middle of September, as there would then be time for it to get fairly strong before the winter sets in.

Management of Breeding Gilts.—The gilts picked out for breeding can be kept for some time the same as cut pigs. They should be fed so that they are kept in good store condition, and cannot be kept too well if they do not get fat. By giving liberal diet they will be larger at twelve months old than some that are allowed to go short will at sixteen months. They are also best with plenty of exercise, as they grow straight and strong in muscle and frame, and will not get so soft and flabby as when shut up altogether. The gilt intended for breeding should have for staple food—till it has been weaned at least a month—good middlings twice a day, and a little hard corn once a day will do it good. It may then have a little bran mixed with the middlings, and given so by degrees till it has half bran and half middlings. As it gets older, its feed should be given according to what it obtains elsewhere. If on a farm, it may pick up nearly enough corn to keep it. With a cotter, it may have the run of an orchard, and get some grass or roots or odds-and-ends. But green food only is not good enough for a growing gilt, and it must have an addition given it, according to the judgment of the owner. If it has plenty of grass and roots and a little hard corn, peas, or beans, or maize are good. But it must be kept growing from the time it is weaned till it pigs, and at the time it comes down to pig should be quite fresh.

Hogging Gilts on.—There is much controversy as to the proper age at which the gilt should be hogged on. If kept well and growing I should let it go at eight months. I have had them hogged on considerably under that age, and they have turned out good mothers. But I should certainly hogg them on by the time they are eight months, unless they would come down at a better time by running on longer. If they are kept well, and are from good growing stock, and the owner wants them to pay him well, eight months is better than older. It is best with gilts to have several together, and hogg them on with a boar of one's own. This a farmer or considerable breeder can do, but a man with only one or two must take them to a boar, and it is often a good deal of trouble to get them hogged on, as they cannot be noticed like a sow.

Some owners often have a deal of trouble to get gilts to come in season. If there is any difficulty in this way it is a good plan to change the diet. If they are being fed on cool and washy foods, as roots, bran, &c., substitute some barley meal, maize, or beans; but barley meal is the best, and if fed rather liberally on this for some time it will usually bring about the desired result.

When they are hogged on they may be kept as before, and by the time they are coming down they should be in good order. Over-feeding is not likely to predispose a gilt to milk fever, as it might a sow.

The Sow to Buy for Profit.—The other way of obtaining good stock, as I mentioned, is by buying a sow from a litter of pigs. It can then be seen what her true value is. Empty sows vary in price: small and bad sorts may sometimes be bought at 45s. or 50s. Good ones vary, as a rule, between 60s. and 70s. At the time of correcting this, sows are worth but little more than half these prices. But as every pig-keeper endeavours to get his sows hogged on for pigging at the right time, which is about January or February, at that time, being in more general demand, they are worth more. 70s. seems a good price for an empty sow, but I have often seen that given for extra good ones just from a good litter of pigs, the buyers being well aware that the best are the cheapest.

The sow will usually come in season just as the milk is drying up, which happens from a few days to about a week after weaning. They should not be allowed to miss this time, as they are more likely to stand then than if run on another time, which is about three weeks later. But as the breeder may think it better to let her run over a time or two, to pig in a better or more suitable time, this would of course alter the case. The sow should be kept fairly well after weaning, but not on milk-producing foods, rather on something of a heating nature, as barley-meal or whole corn. She will usually be in season for two or three days, and it is always advisable to catch her the latter part of the time. If the owner has a boar let them have a daily run together, and there is no fear of missing. Most sows show when they are in season, but some, on the other hand, if not watched, are apt to be overlooked and go too long, which means loss of time and expense. It is best, therefore, if not noticed the second or third day, to drive her to the boar, and if not ready, to make arrangements with the owner to keep her a day or so, or bring her back, according to the distance. When she has had the boar feed her well, and shut her up securely by herself for a day or two. She should not be allowed to run with any down-pigging sows, as it only excites the latter, and these, by jumping about, may be hurt.

Management of "In Farrow" Sows.—After the sow is hogged on she may be kept at little cost—on grass in the summer, or any green food, clover, vetches, &c.; but it is well, unless she can pick up any loose corn, to give her a few good dry beans, if only half-a-pint a day. Flat maize, when a low price, if scalded or soaked some time before use, are a cheap substitute for beans. With a cotter or small breeder there is often a little wash and odds-and-ends, and if any addition is needed a little bran may be given. A good suckling-sow will come off the pigs low in frame, but by the time she is hogged on a month or two, she will usually get in fair condition. She must be kept all through in fair order, and additional food be given to keep her up to this, so that by the time she has a few weeks to lay she should be inclined to get fresh.

It is a great mistake to keep sows very bad and low in condition till they are within a few weeks of pigging, and then put them on extra good food, and flush them up and get a lot of soft meat on them. If left too long, they cannot get in condition, but will have a flush of milk which may turn out disastrous.

Management when Farrowing.—Over-feeding a sow with milk-forcing foods, when she is ready to come down, will cause an abundant supply of milk. The better suckler the sow is, the more dangerous it is for her to have an attack of milk fever, which I shall treat of further on. Good mothers and free sucklers are the most delicate in constitution, and suffer the most when this does attack them, and it should be the breeder's aim to prevent it if possible. Its cause is redundance of milk. For the last week before her time is up, especially if she be bagging fast, she should be kept short of food and have liberty to take gentle exercise. Whilst pigging, she should not be over done with food, nor for a few days after when the danger will be over. A little opening medicine given after she has pigged, if her bowels appear costive, will help her a good deal. The sow must then be kept, so that she is in good order, fresh but not over-fat, and no difference made in her diet before pigging, except to keep her a little short before her time is up—say a few days or a week. With gilts, if they appear rather short of milk, a little better food may be given. They should be shut up at night in the place intended to pig them in, for two or three weeks before their time is up. They may be given a fair amount of litter, and as the time comes on they will get it up in one corner, pull it to pieces, and get it short and soft, which is what is required.

When sows get within a day or so of pigging (and they generally pig about the day 16 weeks from when hogged on) they should be watched, and if they have any inclination to carry a lot of litter into their stye, they should be shut up. They are best left alone, and little food given at a time. From the time the first pig arrives, a good sow will lie down till she has finished and cleansed, but many will be up and down all the time, and it is in the latter case that attention must be given, to see that none are over-laid. All the straw should be moved except a little, but that which is taken out should not be thrown away and wasted, but reserved for afterwards.

The *most suitable* persón to attend to the sow is the regular attendant, as often no one else would be tolerated, and in some cases not even him, as some sows, however quiet they may be at another time, are so savage at anyone being near that it only excites them to become worse. and instead of saving the lives of any, may be a cause of her trampling on them. When it is found this is the case, no one should go near her. But this is one case out of twenty, and the sow that flies at her young and kills them is an exceptional one. If the sow appears quiet, she may be approached from behind and gently spoken to, and scratched under her leg behind; and it will always repay for the trouble, if she proves fairly gentle and quiet, to remain with her, or look in every five or ten minutes.

As soon as each pig is born, if it does not quickly find its way to the teat, it should be guided there, taking due care not to make it squeal so that the mother jumps up. As soon as it gets to the teat and takes a little milk, it will quickly get strong, but if, in cold weather, it gets away from the mother for only five or ten minutes and gets cold, it loses all energy in looking out for the teat, begins to squeal, and cannot be got to suck. The chief thing, then, is to keep the sow lying down, and get each one to the teat as soon as born.

A sow may begin to pig when one's attention is being given to something else, or in the night; and when next seen there may be several at the other side of the stye half dead, or perhaps quite, which might have been prevented if help had been handy. Some sows will get up and down all the time while pigging, and be likely to lie on any; if one is laid on, it will begin to squeal; or she may pop down on one and soon suffocate it, if not moved. In this case she should not be used harshly, or hit, or kicked, as this will only make her ill-tempered, but gently pushed up, and the pig got out and placed against her udder.

Many sows will pig by themselves without any help, quite as well as if anyone was near. But if five out of six were to do this, it would not prevent an interested man, whether owner or attendant, from being handy to render help if needed. I have myself sat up all night with a sow which did not pig till the next day, and then would have been as well by themselves as with my help. On the next occasion when a sow was expected to pig, I have huddled in the blankets on a cold night, and found ten or twelve good-sized pigs half perished in the morning; and instead of having the pleasure of tending ten or twelve good pigs with the mother, had the mortification of bringing up five or six only. With the closest attention, however, a sow may bring a good lot of pigs, and part be lost, but there are many litters which might have been larger if attention had been given at this time. Some breeders nail a rail round the outside of the stye, about a foot from the ground, and a little way from the outside, which prevents the sow squeezing a pig against the wall. The stye should be of sufficient size for the sow to lie down either way and turn about, and of course must be larger for a big sow than for a small gilt.

As soon as the sow has pigged, she should commence to cleanse. This should be taken out of the stye, and the sow not allowed to eat it; whether it does them harm or not is not the question, as it may entice the sow to eat a weakly pig or any poultry afterwards. Dead pigs should also be removed, as most sows will eat them, and this should be avoided. When she has finished, she will get up and look out for some food. Little should be given at a time, and nothing is safer than bran with a few toppings or middlings, the bran keeping her bowels open. At the first feed after pigging the sow will be hungry and inclined to be ravenous, and this is a good opportunity to give her a little opening medicine, as it is much better that she should be kept a little relaxed than otherwise. She should be fed a few days on this plan, keeping her slightly hungry, and about the fourth day if feeding well, both danger to herself, and to the pigs in getting over-laid, may be considered over. Indeed, it is seldom, provided the sow is in good health and goes on all right, that she lies on any pigs after she has had a feed and lies down. Part of the bedding taken out may now be put in, and the remainder if she seems careful; but it is well not to provide any long fresh straw, or to remove the bed where she pigged, for a few days at least.

Milk Fever.—It is the free milking sow that is most likely to be attacked with milk fever. These sows are the most delicate in constitution. It is seldom a bad suckler is attacked, as she will convert any food given her into strength and flesh. All means should be used to prevent it. The cause is an over-supply or redundance of milk, so that the pigs cannot get it away fast enough, and the udder is not cleared out. The outlet then is stopped, the bag gets hard, and the milk is penned back on the sow, which causes her bowels to become costive, a complete stoppage often ensuing.

I have said that over-feeding a sow when the milk is coming often proves disastrous with a free milker. Keep the sow, then, short a few days or a week before pigging, and for a few days after, *and this will lessen the danger.* But some sows will convert everything to milk, even if treated in this way.

For days before pigging some sows will have a tremendous udder, and on a short-legged sow this will almost drag the ground, and by the time she farrows will begin to get rather sore and hard. Such a case as this must not be neglected. Twelve hours' neglect after pigging may be a source of trouble and loss. The pigs must be induced to get out what milk they can, and if the udder is very hard it should be well rubbed with soft soap and warm water, and got soft, and some lard rubbed in well. I have myself got out what milk I possibly could and continued this treatment till the udder has got right. There cannot be much done unless the bag is very stoney and hard, for twelve hours at least; then, if it is not limper and appears hot and feverish, the sow must not be neglected, *especially if she refuses to eat at proper meal time*, and does not let the pigs suck with a draught. She will lie on her belly, and appear unconcerned whether they are laid on or not. Letting her out to gentle exercise without exciting her will do her no harm, but rather the reverse. If she has a free passage in the bowels and the excrements is not lumpy and hard, there is not much to fear, but if, on the other hand, she passes nothing, or only a little, which is very hard, and appears listless, and wanting to lie down on her belly, then all means must be used to get her to take some strong relaxing physic —cattle salts or castor oil. A sow in this state with a regular stoppage requires a large amount of medicine before the bowels can be got to move, and if the lives of pigs or sow are valued, timely means must be taken to give some medicine. If she will not eat anything, or no medicine is eaten in the food, then she must have some forced down her throat. The means of doing this without choking her I will explain further on.

The case of a sow dying or losing her pigs with milk-fever will be very rare if proper care be taken. It is more often the case of misplaced kindness than anything. A breeder may pig a good many sows, perhaps, before he has a case, and many reading this may think I am dwelling on the subject with unnecessary length, and going into details more than is needed. I think not, because, although a man may pig a good many sows and have no trouble in this way, yet he may lose one litter, and be £2 or £3 out of pocket, and a sow and pigs worth perhaps £5 or £6, through not having timely warning. I should have been glad of a little friendly advice in my time, but I had to learn by experience, and pay for it.

In the middle of one summer, when I was quite a lad, I had two fine large white sows in-pig, about the second litter. Either by carelessness or false economy (I forget now which, but think the latter), I kept these sows rather short of food. About two or three weeks before their time was due to pig I awoke to the fact that they were rather low in condition. Thinking to get them on before they pigged, I began to feed them on some good middlings, as much as they could eat, twice a day. The consequence was that a week or more before pigging they had tremendous udders, and by the time they were down could hardly move. I looked at this in a very different light from what I have looked at a similar case since, and did not concern myself till they farrowed. One farrowed with about twelve fine large pigs, which did anyone good to see them. The mother had such abundance of milk that it squirted away from her whenever she moved. About twenty-four hours after pigging she refused her food, the udder got hard and hot, and she lay on her belly and would not let the pigs suck. For some days she ate nothing, the pigs getting poorer and poorer, and getting laid on or dying one at a time. Nothing passed through her all the time. She became so weak that at last she could not get up herself without help, and then staggered to a trough and sucked down a little drink. I at last, with a little help, got some physic down her, and got her bowels to move. The udder by this time had dried almost up. When I once got something through her she began to pick up a little green food and suck a little warm milk, and when the turn had come she began to go on. Four pigs remained, reduced to mere skeletons, and it was grievous to see them about, my only object in allowing them to live being that they might help the mother. They soon got on when the flow of milk returned, and in a few weeks' time were as sleek as moles. The other sow pigged about a week after with a good litter, and became the same, in fact worse, for I lost the whole of the pigs, and would have sold the sow for a trifle. By repeatedly giving her medicine I at last got her bowels to move, but she was reduced from middling condition to a skeleton, and was some weeks before she got round.

Now here were two sows that ought, two weeks after pigging, to have been worth £12, worth not half that sum, and I even then considered myself fortunate in not losing both of them. I had pigged a good many before these, and never saw a case so bad, and may say that, by taking care, I have had but little loss since. I give these instances in the hope that it may save other breeders from such a loss.

These two sows I was inclined to fatten, but being young and really good ones I was sorry to do it. I asked some breeders' opinions, and had, as is often the case, a variety of advice, some asserting that they were most likely to be a trouble next time; some that they were sure to; some that they were no more likely to than any other sows that were free milkers; and some even confidently asserting that they never had it more than once. I should advise anyone in a similar position not to try them again if they had a bad attack. In the case of mine, I pigged them again, and they brought up a score or more of good pigs. I used all caution in feeding and general treatment, but I believe that I should have had trouble if I had not treated them with extra care. I am not going to assert that my treatment is an infallible preventive of milk fever, but I give my experience as a warning against injudicious treatment by over-feeding, &c.

In short, do not keep the sow down poor, and think to get her in condition for suckling a lot of pigs by extra feed a little while before her time is due; but keep her so that she is in good order when coming down. It is well known that all animals will do best when they are in young, nature causing them to store up strength and flesh to stand against the strain on the system when they are suckling.

Treatment of Suckling Sow.—When the sow has farrowed a few days or a week, and is found to be going on all right, her bed should be cleaned out well. It is a good plan to throw down a little lime, but so that the pigs do not get it in the feet. They should then be kept well littered up with good wheat straw if possible, but barley straw will do if it is shifted often. The bedding and everything should be moved every few days, or once a week at the longest, and fresh given. It pays well to do this, as it keeps the pigs better on the skin and in healthier condition than if allowed to lie on a stale bed. On a farm there is no difficulty in keeping them in good abundant bedding, and with straw at the present low price of about 20s. per load it would be false economy to keep them short. When straw cannot be purchased under about 1s. per truss of 36lb. or upwards, then a farmer is naturally anxious to market what he can, while a cottager or anyone who buys it must be careful not to waste any. But a truss of straw a week is not a great deal with a lot of pigs. In the cold weather they must be bedded up well, but during the summer months they may be kept with less. Wet or damp straw must on no account be given, and as much care should be taken in this respect as one would take in seeing that they themselves sleep in a warm and dry bed. Husk, cold, or cramp is sure to follow the use of damp bedding.

The *best and cheapest* food for a sow with pigs is good fine toppings or middlings, with an admixture of bran, and there is nothing safer. The toppings of themselves are apt to be too sticky, and a little bran added will keep the bowels in order and will be a better food. One part of bran to two or three parts of toppings, more or less according to the number of pigs the sow has, and how she is suckling down, should be given. If it is a large sow with only five or six pigs, then she must have more bran and less toppings, unless she is getting old or is not a good breeder; then, if the season is right, it may be advisable to feed her well, so that by the time the pigs are ready to wean, she will be nearly ready for killing. In the case of a free milking sow with a good litter, she cannot be kept too well; but it must be borne in mind that always having a trough full of food is not feeding well, but is only a slovenly way of feeding, while nothing is worse for a good sow. It will cause her to get dainty and off of her stomach quicker than anything. A sow should be given only as much as she will clear up at each meal. Feed her twice each day, as early in the morning as possible, and as late at night as convenient —not sometimes at 6 a.m., sometimes at 8 a.m., sometimes at 3 in the afternoon, and sometimes at 6. Six o'clock in the morning and 6 o'clock at night would certainly be best; but in the winter this would be impracticable, and it must be managed according to other work. Seven o'clock in the morning and 4 or 5 o'clock in the afternoon during the winter would be reasonable times, but regularity should be practiced. The sow will know when the time comes, and if delayed long she will be on the fidget, and do herself a deal of harm. The following is a good routine: Fed in the morning between 6 and 8 o'clock, the sow should be left for a few hours at least to rest undisturbed with her pigs. Then, unless the weather is very rough and cold, let her out for an hour or so, and then turn her in with her pigs. In the middle of the day she should be given another feed if she has a good litter and is suckling down. Many feeders like to give the ordinary feed at this time, but I prefer to give a little green food—mangolds if they are ripe and good, late in the spring—a few carrots, vetches, or clover, according to the time of the year, as some green food will keep her in health and appetite. If she is getting down very weak and low, a few good dry *old* beans will do her a lot of good and keep her up. Not many are needed—about a pint or so, according to the size of the sow. She may then be with the pigs till the afternoon's feed, or be let out for another hour or so, according to the weather—when the weather is warm she would be best out again. Then the afternoon's feed, and be left for the night. In giving the afternoon's feed, except in cold frosty weather, enough should be given, and if a little is not quite cleared up, no harm will be done, as it is longer till the morning; but a large quantity must not be left. The first meal in the day it is well to give only just sufficient—so that she could eat a little more. It cannot always be given to a nicety of course, but a clean trough should always be kept through the day.

Getting Pigs to Feed Early.—Till the pigs are two or three weeks old, if well done, they will not do much more than lie and sleep, and they should be fat and sleek. Previous to this age they are as little trouble as at any period—keeping them well and fresh-bedded, and feeding the sow carefully, will be the only work. By the time they are three weeks old they will become possessed of a desire to see a little more of the world than their limited bed. They will come round the trough and begin to smell about, as if they would like to have a taste. It is now that the most attention must be given, and *a good deal of the success in pig-breeding depends on getting the pigs to feed in good time.* In the litters of various sows there is much difference in the time they begin to feed, varying between three and five weeks as a rule. It is when the sow is let out for her exercise that they should be tempted to begin. A small, shallow wooden trough is as handy as anything. In this should be put a little milk, with the chill taken off and just thickened. By getting them to this a few days, when they appear to want to feed, they will little by little learn to eat. For a week they may not perhaps eat a pint, but they will quickly learn the way, and once started they will be no trouble. A little wheat laid on a flat board should also be put in their way, and as they begin to eat a little, a few dried peas may be substituted. When pigs begin to feed, they generally scour, sometimes more, sometimes less, and the quicker they can be got to feed, the sooner they get over it. The pigs of some sows, as I have said, will quickly feed and be but little trouble, and these scour the least and get on best. On the other hand, some sows' pigs are much more trouble to get to feed, and these generally scour the worst. Some may be got to feed well when about a month old, whilst others are five or six weeks, or even more, before they can feed well. In the latter case, a good deal of trouble must be taken to avoid loss, and if the second litter of a sow were so, I should reject that sow, unless any other cause were noticed. If they scour when the weather is rough and cold, they must not catch cold or get wet, as this would aggravate it, and some might be lost

Exercise for Sucking Pigs.—During the warm summer weather, when the pigs seem inclined to come out of their bed, say, when they are two or three weeks old, let them out to have a run in a meadow if possible. Fifteen minutes or so at first should be long enough, gradually letting them out longer, but not so that they wander about after the mother and get over-tired. By the time they are feeding well, a few hours a day out with the mother will do them a lot of good. It is a good plan, if the styes are situated right, to have a hole, so that the pigs can run in and out as they like into a meadow. They will then lie down when tired, which they would perhaps not do if out with their mother. By the time they are six weeks old, they are best at large, if they do not stray into mischief. It is a great mistake to pen young growing pigs up in a close place, for they are much healthier when running about, and grow much better: any place, so that they are in shelter, will suit them better than the handsome-looking brick places that are "the go" on many farms.

In the cold weather—often up to April and May, we have cold damp weather and cutting east winds—they should not be allowed at large, but should be kept in some good roomy place; but when there comes a warm, genial day it should be taken advantage of to let them out.

Artificial feeding should follow nature as near as possible, and to be successful in pig-breeding one must make a study of the natural instincts of the pigs. The pig in a wild state is a digger. Now, what does he dig for? Many will say for mischief, especially when a strong store pig begins to root up a new-floored sty, just under your nose, or does a little ploughing in a meadow. No such thing. It is no more mischief than our taking salt in our food, or going to a doctor, when we are out of sorts, is mischief. There is no doubt but that in the soil there are all kinds of medicines, vegetable or mineral, to remedy or prevent all the ills the pig is heir to. The pig knows this, and its natural instinct prompts it to dig, just as our common sense prompts us to seek remedies when feeling out of sorts. When a pig gets overdone with food, and is clogged up, he commences to dig for earth, to clear his stomach and digest his food, and if you do not give him some cinders or earth he will soon begin to look out for himself. It is natural for a pig to consume a quantity of earth, and if he is prevented from getting at it, we must supply him with it and take it to his stye. Coals, cinders, or a "spit," or "shovel-full" or two of earth are always welcomed by a feeding or fattening hog, by a sow, or by a young pig. Let a lot of small pigs out of a stye when only a few weeks old, and as soon as they get on grass, or where they can dig, they begin to do so, and if let out they will often find there what we cannot supply them with. When the scour is on pigs, this will stop it quicker than anything; but do not neglect them too long so that they get very bad and weak, or the remedy will come too late, or at least a great deal of mischief will have been done.

The cause of Scour in Small Pigs.—It is sometimes through the sow having an abundance of milk, and sometimes the reverse; sometimes through feeding her on improper foods, which are too heating or relaxing. Improper foods are, damaged or damp corn out of condition; and too many roots—mangold or swedes—must never be given till late in the spring, when they will act beneficially. There are also many cheap and impure feeding stuffs, containing injurious substances. All these things cause the sow's stomach to get out of order, and this will have a bad effect on the pigs.

When suckled down low a sow will often get dainty and unable to feed properly; she must then be fed carefully and often, on the best food. It is the last week or two that the sow is pulled down, and if she was in a low condition when she farrowed, the evil will now be seen. A good milking sow, when she gets down weak and low, will, as I have said, get dainty and off her stomach, and often when like this will seem to have a craving for impure drink; she will go to the drainings of the yard and begin to chew the dung. When this happens, it shows that the stomach is badly out of order, and nothing is better than a good cleansing medicine. A good simple medicine is, about three tablespoonfuls of floury brimstone with a table-spoonful of madder, given about twice a week, early in the morning, when hungry; the feed over-night should be less than the usual quantity, to get her to eat it. Indeed, a little medicine, as above, given once a week from the time the sow farrows till the pigs are taken away, will act beneficially in causing her to throw off any impurities. It is perfectly safe, and although simple, will do quite as much good as many high-sounding patent medicines. If a sow gets very bad with the unnatural appetite as described, some salts may be given with advantage.

As soon as the pigs begin to eat, it is advisable to have a separate place, or if a good-sized stye, a part partitioned off, for them to feed in away from the mother, with a small hole for them to run backwards and forwards. They can be fed on no better food than genuine middlings, twice each day, morning and night, with some good dry peas in the middle of the day. The middlings should not be allowed to get sour in the trough, and only as much as they will clear up should be given them each feed. The peas will help them on, and they will grow stronger than if only stirred food is given. But they should not be overdone, as there is such a thing as young pigs doing too well, and having fits through eating too many peas. For a litter, say, of ten pigs, give as many as they will eat, up to about a pottle or half-peck per day; these will do them good, whilst many over might do them harm. If not running out in a meadow, the young pigs should be given some green food, cinders, coal, earth, &c., occasionally.

How to use other Foods for the Suckling Sow and Pigs.—The kind of food I have just recommended is the best, safest, and cheapest that can be given. I should advise anyone who has to buy all his pig food to use this as the staple food. There are many waste foods, however, that can be utilized for the suckling sow, but they must be given with care. Barley, if dry, may be given in a small proportion, say one-third to two-thirds of the same weight of dan or bran. The only economy in giving it is that there is no sale for it, and that it cannot be turned into money in any other way. Even then I should not give it to sows, if I had any other feeding pigs. If given, it must be the thin screenings from good dry barley, and should have no injurious substances with it.

THIN SECONDS GOOD DRY WHEAT.—If there is no sale for this elsewhere and no other pigs to consume it, it may be ground and given in small proportions, say about one-third or one-fourth with other food. For instance, 1 quarter each of this wheat, barley, middlings, and bran, will make a good feed for the suckling sow.

OATS are no doubt a good and safe milk-producer, but they must be very cheap to be used in any quantity. Neither pea- nor bean-meal should be used, unless perfectly dry; I would not advise anyone to use them even then largely, as they are apt to be too heating, and are generally too dear according to other foods.

MAIZE I should not use here, except in very small proportion to other foods. Exceeding cheapness, compared with other foods, would be the only temptation for me to use them.

RAW POTATOES are but very little use for a suckling sow, and boiled ones are not to be recommended. A few may do no harm, but I should not give many. They soon begin to ferment, and unless they are cooked fresh at each meal may do the sucking pigs harm.

MANGOLDS should not be given till late in the spring, when they are very good for a sow as milk-producers.

TARES, clover, grass, cabbage, or any green food used as an addition will always do the suckling sow good.

PRICKLY COMFREY is a fine thing for pigs of all ages and descriptions. It takes them a little time to get used to it, but when once they do take to it, they are fond of it, and it is a fine thing to keep them in good health. I have had both sows and pigs when unwell eat a few leaves of it in preference to anything else. On all farms—where a quantity of pigs are bred—a rood, or even a few poles, will be found extremely handy.

ACORNS should not be given to the suckling sow, and should be given very sparingly to pigs when shut up, and not at all till they are thoroughly ripe, or they may lead to mischief. They are best thrown down, so that the pigs can pick them up themselves. When pigs run about and pick them up under the trees, they naturally consume a good deal of earthy matter, and seldom hurt. It used to be the custom in parts where there were many oak trees, for the farmer to purchase a few good strong pigs in harvest time, or let his "own breeding" run about and get their own living in the stubble; and when this was over the acorns began to fall, on which they then lived, and he thus got some good strong stores ready to consume a quantity of meal and be finished off. In consequence, however, of the low price of feeding-stuffs and other causes, this is not carried out so much now-a-days, and on many farms where a drove of hogs used to be running the fields and meadows, it is now quite discontinued.

A sow with young pigs running about a meadow and picking up a few acorns will not hurt, but she should have enough good food to keep her from being hungry enough to eat a quantity. All meals or offal given to the sow must be given in pure water. No stagnant water, or water that is contaminated by any drainings from the yard, should be used. The food should be stirred thicker in cold weather than in the hot summer. It is a good plan always to let the sow have a chance to drink some pure water or to get at it at least once a day. If she gets thirsty and cannot do so, she will drink any impure water she can get at. This, of course, should not be allowed, and where the sows get out together, a trough should always stand with pure water in it, or they should have some given in the middle of the day, especially when it is hot.

Warm Foods.—Some feeders would give the sow her food warm, but where this is once begun it must be carried on, and would not be practicable, except in the case of a man who only keeps one or two. The young pigs, when they begin to feed, will no doubt be better with the food stirred in warm water, and it would repay anyone who has plenty of time to do this during the cold months of the year ; but before beginning it, consider that they will badly miss it when left off. Just to get them to pick up a little, for a few days it may be slightly warmed, and then, when they are fairly started eating, leave off, and it will not be missed. But I advise anyone to consider what extra labour it means to give any quantity of warmed food. They will do very well with it stirred in cold water if fed right. There is nothing better to help pigs on, when with the sow, than milk, the true value of which for pig-keeping is hardly appreciated. But if a large quantity is given, and then not any, they will miss it for a while

Weaning.—The time of weaning pigs varies from eight to ten weeks old as a rule ; they are sometimes taken away earlier and sometimes later, but the time mentioned is the most reasonable. In the cold weather it is advisable to let them remain with the mother longer, to get thoroughly strong, as if taken away too early they do not move along for a while. It should depend a good deal on the time they have been feeding, and in the case of any that have been late before they commenced, they should be kept with the mother longer. I usually like to see them with the mother in the summer till they are nine weeks old, and in the cold weather till they are ten weeks. They should then be good pigs and well able to take care of themselves, and as a rule will do as well without the mother as with her. The state and condition of the sow should also in a measure be a guide to weaning, as sows that are pulled down very weak have usually done the pigs extra well, and these pigs would be best taken away in fairly good time; on the other hand, if the sow is strong and well and the pigs are doing well, they may be left a while longer. Some sows do the pigs well till they get six or seven weeks old, and then are useless through the milk drying up, when they are best away; but such sows should be rejected for breeding, as this fault will become worse the more litters they have. But if a sow has a cold and gets off her stomach for a day or two, or is unwell through any cause, her supply of milk may be lessened; she should not be rejected, as her milk will usually return all right. It is when the sow is hardy and feeding well, and yet appears to have no milk about her, that it is a fault. A profitable sow should have as good a supply of milk as ever when the pigs are nine or ten weeks old.

There are some sows faulty in other respects. For instance, they may have a large quantity of milk, but of such inferior quality that the pigs, although they get a bellyful, look poor and bad and do not get on; these sows should also be culled out. Some sows bring a good-numbered litter, but irregular in size, some being good-sized ones and others not much bigger than rats. It will soon be seen if the sow is at fault by the udder—if the teats the small pigs suck from are light and do not contain much milk. *The favourite sow* should be the one that brings a good level lot of pigs. The first litter of a sow is nothing to go by with regard to numbers, as I have known good breeders bring two, three, and four at first, and afterwards turn out well.

The gilt should be judged by the way she suckles her first lot; if she brings only a few up well, all right; but supposing she has five or six, part good pigs and part very small, I should not look upon her with a very favourable eye. If she brings, say, seven—six good level ones and one small one—then she may be set down as fairly promising; but about seven or eight good strong pigs would be better. A gilt's pig, although they may not be so well grown as an older sow's, should look well on the skin when ready for weaning. A good gilt, if in fresh condition when she farrows and brings up seven or eight pigs or upwards, by the time the pigs are ready to take away should be pulled well down, or she is not much good for business.

A sow is usually at her best from the second to fourth or fifth litter; but there are exceptions to this rule. Some sows will do the pigs well for about two litters, and then gradually get worse, while others will bring up eight or nine litters without any apparent depreciation in suckling qualities. But it is advisable not to keep them on too long, for several reasons, that I will explain. As soon as a sow begins to get her pigs small or unsizeable, she would be best sold or fatted off, and even though she may do well for seven or eight litters, there is always more danger of an old sow having the milk fever or going wrong when farrowing than a younger one.

I once had a sow that was an extra good breeder. The first litter I had from her was about the second or third; she brought up fourteen good pigs, and for four or five times more brought up regularly the same number. I had eight or nine litters from her, I think, altogether. The last few were about ten or twelve, but never less than ten. The last time, she had twelve as good strong pigs as one could see anywhere. I had made up my mind it should be the last, intending then to fat her off; but I never had the chance, as she was taken ill when the pigs were a few days old, and in spite of all I could do for her, died in a few days, really from no cause except old age, as she was very weak from the time the pigs were born.

She was a sow that paid well, and had something of the Suffolk white breed in her. I never had one to do her pigs better or with less trouble; they hardly ever scoured, but began to feed without any trouble, and always went and did well. They were not the largest growing sort, but they always prospered. This sow, although a good milker, by the time she was coming down up to the last looked like a young one, her udder drawing up close when in pig, and no one would at first sight have thought her to have had more than a few lots, if they had not noticed her tusks, which were as long as a young boar's. A breeder then should keep the sows on, whilst they do well, till they have had five or six litters; then, if tempted to do so much longer, let him take a lesson from the foregoing instance.

Castration and Spaying.—Pigs should be castrated when seven or eight weeks old, and then allowed to lie with the sow till they get thoroughly over it. I advise everyone to have their sows spayed, except those that may be picked out for breeding. It may make no difference if they are to be killed at small weights of 60lb. or 80lb., but, as a feeder may alter his mind, or find a bad trade for small porkers when they are ready to kill, whilst they may be in more demand if fed on longer—he might have cause to regret that he had neglected to have the sows spayed. It is wrong to say that sow pigs will always do as well not spayed as when spayed, and no one who has personally attended to and fed a quantity but will have been thoroughly convinced of the loss in fatting unspayed sow pigs on to great weights. Some sow pigs are certainly different from others in this respect, as those out of some litters will do as well unspayed as spayed, and scarcely worry at all. But this is the exception; as a rule, when they once begin to come in season, they are on the worry for at least three or four days, and sometimes nearly a week. They refuse their food, are continually up and down the stye, and not only are they wasting time and food themselves, but are raking about and will not let the cut-hog pigs rest; in fact, one sow pig left in a litter will annoy the remainder and give them no rest; and by the time they are ready to kill there is always a lot of waste, especially if the right time for killing is not selected. The charge for the operation is trifling—about 2d. or 3d. per head—whilst it means shillings in the owner's pocket. By the time they are worth 30s. or 40s. apiece, I should value unspayed sow pigs at least 2s. or 3s. a head less for my own fattening.

There are many parts of the country where spaying sow pigs seems almost unknown, or, if known, is but little practised. It is more through neglect than anything, although it may be in a measure because there are no practised hands to do it. It is an operation that requires a good time to learn before anyone can operate with safety, and for this reason it is not practised as it might be. As a rule it falls to the lot of the general castrator. When once it is learned, it can be done with perfect safety. One objection that is raised to the operation is that it is dangerous, and that losses may occur. In answer to this, I can only say that out of the large numbers that I have had operated upon, I have had but very few cases of pigs dying or being injured, and these would not have occurred if I had used the care I should have done in seeing to the pigs; in short, through my own neglect in not properly fasting, &c. Instructions as regards this I will mention presently. Another objection is the pain it gives to the pigs—unnecessary pain, some will state. The operation certainly takes a little longer than cutting the boar pig, and if the noise the pig makes is in proportion to the pain, then it is bad; but when we remember how a pig will squeal and make a noise any time it is caught for ringing, moving, &c., I think this objection may be overruled.

Pigs should fast at least twelve hours before they are operated upon, and at least twenty-four hours after, and for the next twenty-four hours should be fed very sparingly. If this advice is fully carried out no harm will accrue to them. A pig cannot be operated on safely when it is full, and most operators would object to spay a gilt unless it was quite empty; so that anyone who has gilts to spay must make arrangements with the castrator, so as to fast them before he comes. As a rule, he will advise the owner to keep them well fasted after he has left; and, of course, a sensible experienced man will do so; but many men who have charge of pigs, or even the owner of them, may think they will hurt by the fast, and plead to give them "just a little" when they are done, and, although instructed to give none that day, make up their minds to give *a little* in spite of the advice. The result is that the pigs are a much longer time in healing, and do not get over it nearly so quickly as when thoroughly fasted. Many heedlessly give the usual amount of food the same night, and if they lose their pigs, or any get injured, have none but themselves to blame.

The operation of cutting boar pigs is easy enough, and it can be safely done; but, as I mentioned with the sow pigs, you require a practised hand. A rough lanky sow-pig is easiest to spay. The best bred broad-backed fleshy pigs are much more difficult to do, and when too young there is a fear of the bed breaking and not cutting clean. The pigs should be well littered-up and kept warm in the winter, but if the weather is mild they are best running about. They may suck the mother as usual, but must have no additional food, and should be shut away when she is fed.

Ruptured Pigs.—These, if bad, are simply a nuisance. It would be better if all breeders made it a rule to kill them for roasters when a month or so old. They are never safe to keep on feeding, and although they may do as well as the others, there is always a fear of losing them, especially when shifting about. If only slightly ruptured, they sometimes get over it, and it is hardly noticeable. They should always be cut with the others if any are left, but should be done by a practised man, as the cut must be sewn up when the stone is taken out.

What to make of Pigs at Weaning.—When the pigs are taken from the sow, it is for the owner to decide whether he will sell them or feed them on. If the former, it is advisable to sell them off the sow when they are at their best. But if they are of good age, and good growing sorts, they will do as well when weaned as when with the mother. If he has a good lot of pigs, they will pay him to sell, or pay him to keep on. But if the sow has not suckled them well, or they are not good growing sorts, then he will find it difficult to get a customer at even a low price; and they will be kept a long time before he gets any return for his money. (See my remarks on Breed of Pigs, page 12).

If he intends running them on, he must ask himself the question, What shall I finally do with them? Make them into small porkers, or run them on as stores and growers and then fatten them, or sell them when worth 30s. or 40s. each for some other feeder? Room and convenience should decide this; or whether he has any more sows coming down soon, so that he will want the styes for them, &c., &c. If he thinks he has room, then whether he would find it more profitable to make them into small porkers of about 60lbs., 100lbs., or for consumption, for trade at home or in the nearest towns, and use his judgment as to whether the price likely to be obtained will give him a fair chance of profit.

He may have a quantity of milk, and think it cannot be utilized better than in making the pigs into small porkers of about 7 stone (8lb. to a stone) and upwards.* We will, then, treat of the management of feeding the newly-weaned pigs into porkers.

Porkers.—*System of feeding for the first few weeks after weaning of small weights.*—A good-growing pig will turn itself into profit quicker than a slow-growing one. A large rompy pig is not suitable. A good cross between the White Yorkshire and the Berkshire is as good as any. Many would

* Fattening porkers for the London market has not been profitable of late years, as a large quantity of pigs from abroad have kept down the prices. The latter, although of much inferior quality, make almost as much as prime corn-fed English pork, and are passed off as such. Till there is a combination of feeders to have their own salesmen to sell only guaranteed English produce, genuine well-fed stuff will stand no chance of fair competition.

prefer the Berkshire only, but I like a cross best. The young pigs must be kept not only growing but fat and sleek from weaning time. If milk in any quantity is given there will not be much trouble to do this, and with milk it will be safer to use a quantity of meal. Good middlings—the same that they had hitherto been fed on—morning and night, with a few dry peas in the middle of the day; in fact, treat just the same as when with the sow. If they had been used to running about, then if you can conveniently do so, let them out for an hour or so every day. But as I may have to include the man who buys pigs to fatten into porkers, and who has not the convenience to let them out, then I can only say, "See that the pigs are supplied with plenty of green food, cinders, earth, &c., as they would get if at large."

There is no doubt but that they will miss the exercise they may have been used to, and if they do seem to get a little dainty and off their feed, if you have only a little back-yard you can let them out for half-an hour every day, and it will do them a lot of good. I am here thinking of my town friends, or rather those in the suburbs of a town, who have but limited room. It is of no use to tell them to let the pigs run out in a grass orchard for half-an-hour or an hour every day.

For about a month the pigs may be fed on the middlings and peas. The middlings may be stirred in cold water, if there is nothing else, but any house-wash odds-and-ends will help them on.

Injurious Substances in Waste Pig Foods.—Be careful that there is no injurious substances in what is used. Many feeders collect their neighbours' house-wash, or contract with eating-houses, refreshment-room and hotel proprietors, and for the waste of certain manufacturers. One injurious substance is salt or brine, and many pigs are no doubt unwittingly killed with this. Salt in a small proportion will not hurt a pig, but rather prove beneficial, and some pig-keepers mix a little in the food. I would not advise any inexperienced pig-keeper to use it except he gets personal advice, which would only be useful at the moment and on the spot. Salt or brine *in large quantities* is deadly poison to a sow or to any pigs, and in feeding on waste matter care should be taken that there is not enough to cause any serious injury. Another injurious substance in waste matter is common washing-soda, if given to a large extent; and others that would, if not kill a pig, make it very ill, are no doubt likely to get into many waste matters.

Finishing-off Porkers.—When the pigs have been weaned about a month, they may have a little meal mixed with the dan. Buying all the food, nothing is cheaper than good genuine foreign barley to finish off with. Good barley only, ground into meal, has recently been fetching 28s. and more per quarter, of 8 bushels, 48lb.; but this price is gradually receding, till we may hope it will soon reach the figure at which it stood in 1889-90, viz., 22s. Inferior dirty and adulterated sorts may be bought for less, but the best is of course cheapest, and should be obtained. This meal may be mixed at first in the proportion of one-third to two-thirds of middlings, by degrees working it to half-and-half, and by the time they weigh 7 stone they should be given two-thirds meal. If kept on much longer, they may be given nearly all meal, but a little middlings will do them good. The middlings are cool—barley is heating—and for this reason, too much barley-meal, when very young, is apt to overheat the pigs and make them break out or turn bad on the skin. By giving it by degrees as they get older and stronger, they will take no hurt. The peas must be given in moderation, commencing for 8 or 10 pigs with a pottle per day, and by the time they are ready to kill, half-a-peck or more may be given.

I have here mentioned middlings and good barley-meal as the cheapest and best foods to buy. Let us consider the others that the feeder will have to buy or has to use up.

Good English barley is of course superior to foreign, but malting barley is too dear, and none will be available except the screenings of this or weathered barley. Weathered barley may be given with advantage if it is dry, but as a rule it will be found too damp to use without due care. It must be ground often and used when fresh, as if allowed to stand any time it is apt to heat, and quickly too, in the sacks. It is best shot down in a bin and moved about till used.

Wheat can only be used when very cheap, and the seconds and screenings or wheat draggings only can be used profitably, or any that has become damaged as to be unfit for flour. Wheat must be used in small proportions to other foods—about one-fourth is quite sufficient; mix this quantity with barley-meal when the pig is a month from weaning, or in a small proportion from weaning will make a very good feed, and will help to force them along. But given in too large quantities it is found to be unsuitable. I have ground the best dry wheat, when it touched the extremely low price of 28s. per quarter, thinking that pigs must do first-class on this; but it would not suit. They did well for about a week, then it seemed too rich; they either ate a lot or refused to eat any, and scoured at times. I reduced it by half, substituting half barley-meal; they then did better, and went on very well. By different trials I have found that they will do better with about one-fourth wheat-meal than with a larger proportion. Oats, beans, and peas are too dear, and are not to be recommended to be ground into meal for pigs.

Maize I should not recommend for small porkers, except very cheap; the meat will not be of good quality, but inclined to be flabby. Boiled potatoes are not suitable for finishing off porkers of small weights. A few given when they are younger would do no harm, but should be given in small quantities. If they are finished off with any quantity in proportion to other foods they will kill light, and the meat will not be so solid as with barley-meal only. It will also boil away more when cooked.

Running on Stores for Large Hogs or for Bacon.—For the first month after weaning these may be treated much in the same way as those for porkers, and they cannot be kept too well. A good many farmers with plenty of yard-room will wean perhaps thirty, forty, or fifty, or even more together, and turn them all into a yard by themselves, where they will be fed more or less regularly till they are thought sufficiently large to sell; about ten or twenty are perhaps picked out at a time, and either shut up to fatten or be sold off. They are perhaps almost grudged the food given them, and are expected to grow and get on on what they can pick up in the straw with the help of a few roots. This is false economy, for a pig taken from the mother and good food and treated in this way for a week or two will rather get of less value than improve. Indeed, I have seen many when weaned a month of less value than when with the sow. When they are once inured to this treatment they are stunted in growth, have a nasty dirty skin, and would even if treated well take some time to get over it. For another three months they begin to grow slowly, especially if they have to fare hard and do not get much trough food, and by the time they are five or six months old may be called rough hardy old stores.

This system of keeping them does not pay the farmer, I am certain. When they thoroughly get over the bad keeping and have attained good bone and frame, of course they are desirable pigs for anyone to shut up and eat a quantity of rough food and to alter. The danger of this is that they alter too quickly, and by being put on to their fill of food too fast are taken sickly; and in many cases, if filled suddenly to repletion for a week on rich food, would be killed. Such pigs as these must be fed by degrees from coarse foods, and be kept short for a week or two; they will then gradually improve and do well.

Young pigs if put together in too large numbers at weaning time, say, as many as forty or fifty in one lot, cannot be fed properly. A pailful of food will be eaten up before the feeder has hardly got the pailful in the trough, and some of the strongest ones will get the lion's share, while the weaker ones will get knocked back, and so be only half fed. About ten to twenty in a lot is better than more. It would pay a farmer to divide his yard off and feed them so, or feed them ten or twenty in a stye, according to its size; and if convenient let them have a run in the farmyard or meadow, some one day and some another, or each at different times of the day. During the cold weather they are best in good warm airy places, with a run out occasionally; but in the summer they would do better under a large lofty hovel or similar place. Treated well, they should be good strong pigs by the time they have been weaned a month. It is always advisable to give a feed of stirred food early in the morning.

Any offal corn that is useless for market may be ground up for them; if thought too heating, a little good middlings may be mixed with it. The morning's feed should now be given sparingly, so that they will clear it up and look for some more. After they have rested a while, they may be let out to have a run where there is any loose corn about to pick up—in the harvest time to pick up the corn littered round the stacks—or taken out on to the stubbles, as the owner thinks well; or they may have a few dirty beans or peas that are otherwise useless given them. These are best thrown down on the ground to be picked up. They will then not bolt them whole. A few roots or a little green stuff may also be given them. At this stage they should always have a good feed at night, when they will lie down contented.

By treating in this manner, feeding well and economically, the pigs will be kept in fairly good order, and will be making the bone and muscle necessary to build the fat on afterwards. They will pay the farmer well for keeping on, not only by eating up his waste out of the way, but also if he bought his food at market or present prices and let them run on as usual. If the farmer does not attend to them himself, he ought to have a good reliable man who will feed them at regular times and with regular quantities, not keeping them short or wasting the food.

The housing and bedding during the summer is not of much consequence, so long as they have a shelter overhead and a dry floor with some litter. They should not be allowed to lie in heating dung at any time, especially in the cold weather, as this will give them a chill when they get in the open, and cause husk and colds quicker than anything. In the autumn, winter, and spring, their bedding and housing should be well attended to. If they lie in a stye with a small yard attached, the bed should be cleaned out well about once a week and fresh dry litter put in. The places should be well shovelled out, and if a little lime be thrown down on the bare bottom before putting in the fresh bed, it will sweeten and do it good. Wheat straw is much the best, especially for pigs just weaned, but barley straw will do if shifted often. If the bed is allowed to lie week-after-week, the pigs will look dirty on the skin, especially if they are not kept fairly well. They will sometimes get a nasty hide-bound skin, which will crack; when they get like this they are termed "stye-baked." They will do no good whilst they remain so, and even by adopting the best treatment they will take a long time to get over it; this is especially the case with young pigs, three months or younger. The styes should be perfectly dry at the bottom, and lie dry round the outsides. (See remarks on Housing).

Pigs kept fairly well in this growing or store state can be sold at any time, or can be fed on fast, for small weights of 15 or 16 stone, or run on longer to make larger hogs.

Feeding Pigs on Potatoes.—Potatoes in a raw state are worth but little to any pigs, but when cooked they may be made profitable under certain conditions. The price of ordinary feeding stuffs and the market price of potatoes should be looked into. With good middlings at about £6 per ton, I should not feed pigs on potatoes; but when middlings are making, say, £8 per ton, and barley-meal in proportion, and ground offal potatoes are only worth 30s. per ton, and small ones 20s., then boiled potatoes may be used profitably, the difference in the comparative prices making them well repay for the trouble and outlay in cooking.

I should not advise anyone to feed a young pig under three months on any potatoes, however, and should give it but little till it was strong. From that time till within about eight weeks of killing them, pigs will pay (if prices are right) for feeding on boiled potatoes. When the pigs get within about eight weeks of killing, they should have the potatoes left off by degrees, and for the last month at least should be fed on good solid meals only. If fed largely on potatoes and killed, they will weigh badly, and the meat will be of inferior quality; but supposing you have been giving a few potatoes and got the pig used to them, they may then be given in the proportion of say a bushel of meal to a bushel of potatoes.

Way to Cook Potatoes.—The potatoes should be cooked at least twice-a-week, and may be mixed in with the meal and water from twelve to twenty-four hours before feeding. There is a lot of work attached to potato-cooking. In the first place, you must have a copper made, if you have not one you can convert into use. The potatoes, if dirty, must be washed, then there is the cooking to be done. A good sharp fire must be kept up, and when they are once on the boil, about fifteen to thirty minutes will do, according to the size of the potatoes; but with a trial or two this can be decided. They are best taken out at once with a perforated jet, put into a shallow tub, well mashed up whilst hot, and then put into another tub for use. If not broken up at the time, they will be much more trouble to do when they get cold and hard. The copper must be well cleaned out each time; also all the utensils, or they will be sticky or dirty for the next use.

The Fattening Hog.—I have mentioned everything about the strong store for bacon till it is worth 30s. or 40s., and have given advice to those who make pig-keeping a business to keep on and sell at about that price, and to keep the pigs in a growing fresh state rather than pinch and half-starve them Buying pigs at about 30s. to 50s. and finishing off for fat pork or bacon, is by many made an industry by itself; we can treat of them either as being kept by a man who has got them up to this price and intends finishing them off for the butcher, or as by the man who purchases at this price to fatten. In Beds. and Herts. those which are not killed for the London markets, at about 6 to 10 stone, are either made into larger pork for home consumption or fattened up for bacon. For home consumption, the demand is for pigs of about 12 stone (8 lb. to a stone) up to 20 stone during the summer, and in the winter from 18 stone up to about 28 stone.

Salt Pork as a Food for the People.—Salt pork has been from time immemorial the staple food of the farm labourer, and who has been in the country with a gang of farm labourers during their out-door meal but has seen them with a hunch of bread and a piece of fat pork of good thickness, and enjoying their meal, as does a townsman his frizzled bacon? It is hardy, good, and cheap, when he can buy the complete fat at 6d. per lb. During the summer, and at harvest and hay-time, he, like everyone else, cannot eat so heartily, and likes it a bit streaky if he can get it, or a piece of butcher's meat; consequently it is not wise to fat pigs up to too heavy weights to come out at midsummer in the country. Now a piece of well-salted fat pork, from a hog fed on good meals, is not to be despised in the middle of winter, when it cuts out hard and solid—certainly being a little streaky improves it. This was the staple food of the forefathers of many an English tenant-farmer, and I know there are many alive now who once had to sit down to a piece of fat pork for dinner; and there is no doubt but that they enjoyed it, and went out to work again with much better will than many of our farmers, who have had a few slices out of a leg of mutton, do now. Happy old times they were, no doubt, in comparison to the worrying "steam-engine"-going days of the present.

But to return to to-day. Pork being the farm-labourers' staple food, it stands to reason that there must be a large quantity fattened, and what are not bought for home consumption are bought by large bacon-curers for their purpose. Now a pig kept fairly well till it gets worth about 40s., can soon be fed on to 15 or 20 stone or more, and would be ready either at that weight or to run on for more. A good-bred pig of the Berkshire and Yorkshire cross makes a good sort for this purpose. But for getting the extra large weights that are made in the north of England, they are best of the Yorkshire type, if slightly crossed, with plenty of frame, and kept in a good growing fresh state till they have formed a frame to grow the meat on. In Beds. and Herts. there are many farmers who purchase them when good strong stores, and do not breed any. These eat up the offal and damaged corn or milk, if any, and make a good lot of high-class manure.

The Fattening Hog as a Fertilizer of the Ground.—The manure, even if a farmer did not gain anything else on the pigs for his trouble, would amply repay him. Yes, it would be a much more sensible way of keeping the fertility in his ground by always having a score or two of hogs fattening, even if he sold all his barley that was fit for malt, and purchased feeding stuffs, than by buying a lot of expensive artificial manures. One way is to be compared with feeding a man on good meat and pudding, and the other giving him a quantity of spirits. On the former he feels fit to do a day's work on the morrow; but the latter only gives him a spirit to use extraordinary exertions and then be all the weaker after. If I am in any way digressing from my actual subject, still it is to the farmer's benefit that he should look upon the hog as a manure- as well as a bacon-producer. Now take our heavy clay lands, for instance; I will guarantee that if a piece of land were drained and cleaned, and then given a good mucking with spit hog dung it would not be exhausted for four or five years.

How to Fatten Pigs.—There is no better way of getting pigs on for the knife than by feeding two or three times a day on good wholesome meals in sufficient quantity to be cleaned up before leaving the trough, and as soon as each meal is consumed, getting the pigs to lie down and sleep. In feeding a lot of strong stores just purchased, they should be brought into the mode of feeding and treatment by degrees. If kept on short commons before, they should have just so much given that they could do with a little more; and if they had been running about before, it would be as well to let them out every day for a little while, just before feeding time; and in putting them off of any rough keep on to very rich food, it should be given with moderation.

During the summer a lot of fattening pigs will do better in an open hovel with plenty of air, and sheltered from the heat, than they would in one of the brick places, as mentioned before. But in such a place as this they would be much better where no other pigs or sows can come near to disturb them. In the winter (provided the place be dry and airy) they would be best in a closer place, and if in the dark it would be quite as well. The chief thing, besides the sorts of food given, is to make the pig happy and contented and satisfied with its position; and everything that causes it to be discontented and to worry should be avoided. For instance, seeing other pigs at liberty; not feeding at regular hours; getting the cold or cramp, to put it in pain; giving too much food to mess about; all these are against its well-doing and ultimate profit. One great thing to hinder a lot of pigs from doing well is to leave the sow pigs unspayed. If there are only two or three, they are sure not only to worry themselves but all the cut-hog pigs as well; and only those who have fattened them—spayed and unspayed, actually feeding them themselves—know what a hindrance this is to their doing well.

It is a custom with some breeders to shut up a lot of stores, in a good roomy place, till ready to come out, and to keep adding litter, and not clear the dung away till they come out, ready to kill. If this is practised during any part of the time, it certainly ought to be all through, for a pig lying in a warm bed, or on the hot dung, and then put in another place, is apt to catch cold. For myself, I think in a good roomy hovel, it is the best way to add litter and not clean them till they are ready to be killed. They should have fresh litter put in a little time before the mid-day meal, as they are sure to turn it about for a while, and will then lie down and rest when fed.

If they are fed in a stye with a yard attached, it is no doubt best to change the bed two or three times a week, throw it outside, and put fresh straw inside.

There is no doubt but that the most suitable food for the pig at this stage is barley-meal; but I think it always advisable, especially at the earliest part, when shut up, to give a little good toppings with it. When purchasing all the food, however, there is no doubt but that barley-meal should be the staple food. I mean meal ground out of sound barley, whether thin screenings or from foreign corn, and not what is often sold as meal, but which contains a good deal of injurious substances. Barley-meal will make better pork than any corn solely used, and if pigs have any other foods mixed to start with, they should be finished off on this. The farmer, of course, must use up his offal corn, and by judiciously blending them together, the pigs will do well.

Milk, of course, produces magical effects in pig-feeding, and it should be given as regularly as possible, not giving a quantity one day and none the next. Given half-milk and half-water, a pig will do better on one quarter of meal than on double the quantity with nothing but water. The feeding of large heavy fattening pigs is the simplest matter imaginable, and yet one man will make them pay when another loses by them. I say feed three times daily—morning, noon, and night—with stirred food the first and last meal, and some whole corn, such as peas, in the middle of the day, this will bring them along as quickly as any way. The mid-day meal should also be supplemented with a little green food and some cinders, coals, or earth. The meals are no doubt best mixed one before another, or twenty-four hours before feeding, in a tub, when it will be more digestible than stirred and given at once. Where a number are fed, it is best to have two or three tubs for the purpose, when they can be cleaned out well before adding more. This food should always be given of about the same thickness. In the summer time many will give it quite thin, especially if milk is added, and in the winter time thicker. My idea is that it is best not given too thick at first, but the last month it is best stirred thick, as it does the pig more good, and does not pass through it so quickly; but a few peas will help to keep the pig together as well as anything.

In the summer, the fattening pig should always have access to a trough of clean water. If the food is then stirred thick, and the pig becomes thirsty, it can have what it wants without taking any hurt; and it is my opinion, by the way I have seen many pigs managed, that they often suffer through not having any water standing by them.

Feeding Pigs on Cooked and Warmed Foods.—Does it pay to have the food cooked? This is a question that often arises among amateur pig-keepers and beginners in general. My experience leads me to conclude that cooking meals does not pay for the extra outlay and trouble it involves, and I would not persuade any feeder to go in for cooking grain, unless he has certain facilities and advantages over the ordinary feeder. Wheat or barley, if cooked at all, should be cooked unground, and it would be the extra cheapness of this grain that would tempt me to cook it; but it could only be carried out successfully where pig-feeding is made a regular business and a number are always feeding, so that a man is always on the spot to do the cooking regularly. On the one side, there is the labour in cooking each day or time, the fuel used, and the erection of proper copper and utensils, to reckon up; and on the other, there is the extra well-doing of the pigs on the same cost of food. I have not tried cooking on a large scale, and would not advise any feeder to go to a great outlay in erecting coppers, &c., as I do not believe there will be that extra weight gained on the pig which will pay for the trouble. Scalding the food by mixing it with boiling water would no doubt be relished by the feeding hogs during the cold months of the year. It must be remembered that once pigs are given their food warm, they must always have it so; but if they do try cooking grain or giving the food scalded continually, then do it on a small scale to start with, say, on one stye of pigs that are intended to come out in a month or so, and feed another stye on ordinary mixed food. It would here be best to divide a lot of pigs that had been treated alike to get a fair result, and reckon up what the actual cost would be on each lot, cost of fuel, and the labour if paid for, as it is on this that the actual cost hinges most particularly, and they will find that the extra outlay will not be repaid when the pigs are killed.

In the case of people keeping 2 or 3 pigs—cottagers, for instance—they often make it a rule to give the food warm; they use the water left in the kettle, and odds-and-ends mixed with it in the pail, and given regularly morning and night; but the actual labour and trouble are put at nothing. I would recommend it in these cases, as the pig is got along faster without any real extra outlay on the part of the feeder.

Cooking Food for Pigs.—Notwithstanding what I have said on page 60, it would answer the purpose of every arable land farmer and market-gardener to have a copper or cooking apparatus, such as Parrish's. There are certain times when potatoes are useless for sale in the ordinary way, and enough are then available to wholly occupy a man's spare time in cooking them. The cooked potatoes would thus only cost the amount expended in labour and fuel.

There may also be other stuffs that would be totally useless except when cooked. Take, for instance, chimblings of wheat, from which the seeds cannot be extracted: pigs will thrive on these when cooked to a jelly. There may also be wheat gone quite musty, so that pigs will hardly eat the meal made from it. This, as well as damp or musty peas and partly-rotten beans, can be boiled up well, and will pay for the trouble. It is in cooking good, sound corn on which pigs will do as well whether whole or ground, in which the labour and fuel are not repaid. Such an apparatus is also handy to boil up potatoes and rough stuff for some little time for old sows, when it is in the way, and so turn it into money. Even if the cooker is not always in use it will be found handy at times, and the original outlay is not great.

The Cottager as a Pig-Keeper.—The thrifty and industrious cottager and labouring man may make one pig, or two or three, pay him as well as any class. And for the encouragement of those who have not tried any, but have always had a disposition, if they could get enough money, to get one in and feed it, by all means try. But if you are going to make it profitable, you must see to it well and not neglect it, and you must have all convenience and room. The sanitary laws are very strict now; the stye must be a certain distance away from any dwelling, so as not to prove a nuisance.

If I had my way, in every village no cottage should be erected unless there was a good piece of ground attached to it. The villages would then be much more healthy, and we should not hear so much of the various epidemics amongst the labouring classes. In many villages the cottages are so huddled together, without sufficient space and ventilation, that they are really not fit to live in. In this connection, I think there ought to be an inspection made before allowing anyone to erect a human dwelling place, and it ought not to be put up on any small piece of ground of just sufficient size for the house without sanitary accommodation. If I am going out of the way of my subject in mentioning this it is because I should like to see in our English rural villages a little less pinching and squalor in the back places. Life should be made a little less arduous for the working man, and a little more sunshine be put into his heart.

My idea of benefiting the labouring classes, is that every steady, persevering, hard-working man should be able to earn enough to live with comfort without getting into debt, and be able to lay a little up for a rainy day. He can barely exist now when in good health and with constant work, and if reverses come or employment fail, then who knows the soreness of an honourable man to find himself slowly but surely driven into debt or starvation? I should like to see him paid a little more, so that he can stand against this. My model of a rural village cottage is a decent house with about 40 or 60 poles or more of ground attached to it, so that if the man is steady and industrious, he can keep a pig or two, and earn a little by that. There is many a man who has raised himself above the common lot of the labourer by beginning in a small way like this, and steadily plodding on, getting first a sow, then perhaps another, and at last a cow. We ought to be proud of such men and try to encourage such thrift. There always will be labourers required to till the soil, and there will always be those content to do this, to work hard and not fare luxuriously—men who would be well contented and satisfied in the position they are in—if they could have a wage on which they could live comfortably, a cottage with a good allotment of ground attached, and a couple of pigs in a stye at the bottom of the garden. These two pigs will eat the odds-and-ends, and the small potatoes will be cooked by the wife and made to go a long way; odd greens and other refuse will also be turned into money in this way. This, with an addition of some dan and a few sacks of meal, will make them some good pigs that will pay all outlay and leave a profit besides.

Any labouring man can at his odd times, more particularly in the summer evenings, soon make a handy little place, large enough for two or three pigs. With a few stout posts and some rough boards, he can soon get the sides put up, then make the roof and thatch it in with a few trusses of straw. Then with a little more rough material he can make a yard outside, and with a little friendly help can get a load or two of chalk and make a good sound dry bottom, which will be ready for the inmates when it is perfectly dry.

Small as this outlay is, I know it is a good deal for men earning about £30 or under per annum to get. Then there are the pigs to buy, and the outlay then must be for other foods, so that it really requires a man of a little capital to get in and finish off even two or three pigs.

We will suppose the man has his stye and everything ready for the inmates, we will also suppose that if he does not want to go to the expense of buying a trough, he will make a strong wooden one; this he can do, and make it answer his purpose as well as an iron one. He must make it strong, with a large foot, so that it cannot be overturned, or else stump it down. He had better nail a piece of iron-hooping or something similar round the edges, to prevent the pigs from gnawing it. His next thought is, what pigs to get. The most useful to him is a good rough hardy pig that has been running a farmyard and has a little age about it, say, one that he can buy for about 25s.; such an one will be able to eat his odds-and-ends up, and will be better than a very young pig just off the sow, especially if it is very early in the spring or getting late in the autumn. Getting into November, he had better have one this age; it will then be strong and well before the winter comes on. Getting into the summer weather, when May has arrived, he can get a young pig, cheaper of course, and will do very well; but one just off the sow, unless it be a very large sort, will be some time before it will consume any quantity of waste matter. It makes much difference in buying one off the sow as to the sort, and I would persuade any cottager rather to give a fair price for a good sort of growing pig, than have a little bad doing sort for almost nothing. Better give 16s. or 18s. for a thoroughly good sort than have a little stunted or small weak one at 7s. 6d. If you can buy the latter it will be on your hands a long while before it moves along, whereas one at about 16s. off the sow will be seen to grow every week, and will weigh 20 stone before the small one will go half as much.

Pig-keeping by the labouring man proves a profit or loss according to the attention and treatment given. I have known pigs purchased at about 20s. each to be kept on till they were worth about 80s., and 20s. each cleared out of them. As a fact, however, I have parted a litter amongst several men, each having two or three. One has made them pay very well, and another has lost by them. What is the reason? One has made a study of his and used up all odds-and-ends to the best advantage; the other has let them go short at one time, and at another has filled the trough full, to be trodden in and wasted.

Pedigree Pigs.—Improving District Inferior Breeds.—On page 20 I have mentioned my objection to giving high prices for in-and-in-bred pedigree boars that have been fed on warm and spiced foods, and got up on purpose for sale and show, and I recommended crossing by getting good boars. I hope readers will not misunderstand me. If I had a quantity of regularly breeding sows, and wanted a well-bred pure one, I would not mind giving a good price for a really good boar from a pedigree herd where animals are fed in an ordinary way—say, for instance, from such a yard as Mr. Saunders Spencer's, a gentleman whose many years of experience, personal attention, and practical knowledge, have secured for his herd world-wide renown. What an improvement would be effected in local breeds if a few such boars or any really well-bred pure Yorkshires, Berkshires, or Tamworths were bought with a little "technical education money," distributed about some counties and let for hire at a low fee by getting large breeders to keep the boars for their own and their neighbours' use, or getting some-one to keep and take the fees by arrangement. I always advise the use of good pure-bred boars, especially with crossed sows.

In Bedfordshire we have some splendid Yorkshire White stock. These crossed with Berkshires, Tamworths, and our crossed sows, produce quality and fattening capabilities to be beaten by none. The produce weigh well when dead, and turn out the right grained meat. Of late years in Bedfordshire well-selected boars have been kept on most farms where breeding is made profitable, and that is the way to keep the pigs up to a good standard and make the sows produce profitable stock for breeding. It is wonderful what one really extra good boar will do for a village where there are a quantity of small breeders. Those who only keep a sow or two have no option but to send to a boar that is handy; and if only one or two inferior or middling ones are available, it makes a vast difference the parish through.

"Technical Education Money" and Smaller Rural Industries.—Of the money spent on technical education and the smaller rural industries, poultry- and bee-keeping, &c., none has been used in instilling in pig-keepers' minds the necessity of breeding from good stock.

Very little money spent in getting some good boars distributed about counties would be quite as well repaid as in anything else, and why so much should be spent on other smaller industries, and the pig totally neglected, I cannot quite understand.

The allotment question seems to be eagerly watched by the working classes, and a large amount of land has been let out in small lots lately. Land is of no use, however, unless well manured, and I do not see, in country places distant from rail, what can better maintain its fertility than pig-keeping. A labourer with a handy piece of ground, a good styc, a good sow, and a good wife, can do himself some good if he can make the best of his pigs when ready to sell. He can also secure a lot of good manure. We might, then, as well have a good paying sort of pig in the country as so many inferior and middling ones.

How Shows Might Improve Breeds.—County and local shows might do a lot of good. Prizes should be offered for farmers', tradesmen's, and labourers' pigs. The points should be: Quality if killed, which can be told by fatted pigs; weight alive for age for pigs, say from eight to ten weeks old off the sows, and various other ages; number of pigs in litters; regularity of sizes of pigs in litters, and weight altogether of litters at various ages. The prizes to be awarded to the most valuable sows for breeding, with symmetry, quality, and weight in the whole litter at certain ages—say, eight to ten weeks (when ready to wean), and other ages after weaning. The sow would then get the prize on the merit of what she can do with good attention. I think milk should not be allowed to be used in feeding, as animals so fed should have classes by themselves; there would otherwise be little chance for poorer pig-keepers, who often see after them best and keep the best stock, but have no milk available. Still, I have seen splendid litters at weaning fed only on cold slop foods and corn. There might also be *selling classes*, or sales of the boars and gilts from such litters might be effected on the ground. Colour and breed should be no consideration in judging: the points should be as mentioned. It is essential to get quick growing and fatting sorts now, in order to make them profitable. This departure from ordinary show-yard systems need not interfere with pedigree and other pure-bred stock. It would do a lot of good by showing how a valuable sow can be made to pay a breeder by good attention, and what weight can be got at certain ages by keeping good stock and by careful breeding; it would stimulate others to keep good paying stock only, and see after them well; and it would also give good opportunities to pig-breeders to secure choice young sows and boars from these litters. I ask local authorities who have the "technical education money" to spend, agricultural societies, show committees, and all who take an interest in our rural industries, to give this matter their consideration. What has been done in improvements of breeds hitherto has been brought about by personal enterprise only.

Irish Pigs.—Irish pig-keepers tell me they have an inferior class of pigs. I have had many orders to send breeding-stock to Ireland to improve their breeds, but I have found that what with the formality to go through, and the expense and trouble involved, the game was not worth the candle, and I have been obliged to decline other orders. Pigs have been practically prohibited from being sent from England to Ireland for a good many years; yet all that time they could be despatched all over England from Ireland without any inquiry, and it seems that English local authorities could not stop them from coming in until November 1st, 1895. Even now, it seems, the Government have no regulation in force as to the animals having come from healthy places and districts in Ireland. Pigs are received at our ports indiscriminately, and can be distributed all over England.

Whilst Ireland sends so many live pigs to England, and the swine fever is there, it is nothing but lunacy to think of stamping it out in England till it has been exterminated in Ireland, *or* until the same method of dealing with it is carried on in Ireland as in England. English pig-keepers, when they are so hampered with restrictions and have to sell at such a loss, have great cause for complaint in this matter, and it is useless to expect their help till this state of things is altered. Of this, however, I will say more further on.

A year or so ago the agricultural editor of the *Times* made the following statement: "Last year we slaughtered in this island on account of swine-fever, and at the expense of the tax-payers, over 57,000 pigs; simultaneously there were sent into Great Britain upwards of 586,000 live pigs from Ireland, where swine fever is rampant. During the last two years the swine-breeding industry in this island has been heavily handicapped by the scheduling of districts, the closing of markets and fairs, and the exclusion from our showyards of the indispensable pig. All this is a costly business, the expense of which has to be borne by the people of this island. To continue the attempt to exterminate swine fever within our shores under such conditions as these is very like trying to fill a bottomless pit."

Diseases in Pigs.—"Prevention is better than cure" may here be forcibly reiterated. Bad housing and bedding, uncleanliness and neglect, are usually the forerunners of the various diseases pigs are liable to, and I cannot say much more with regard to the management in this respect, to prevent these illnesses and complaints, than I have already done. With the human subject, how common is the remark, "only a cold." So with the pig I have heard the same remark. "Your pigs look rather dull, they have a little husky cough." "Oh, they have only a little cold," remarks the owner. But it is "only a cold" that often leads to great losses, and they must not be allowed to remain long with a bad cold on them. If the house, bedding, or anything is likely to be at fault, see to that first; then set to work and get the pig right before he begins to fail. If a pig gets a bad cough on it, or gets the cramp badly, it is best killed before there is a lot of useless money spent on it. But suppose it has only begun to cough, after it is fully ascertained that it lies in a high dry stye and is well bedded, then give it suitable food. Do not give it hot dry food nor a lot of whole corn; but give it a little open purifying medicine occasionally, and when giving this see that it does not get wet or in the cold winds, or it will be best without it.

Cramp, which is really a state of rheumatism in the pigs, is a much dreaded complaint. It is most rife from November to

March. Lying in draughty styes, exposed to the damp and cold east winds, or being moved about in the cold, causes it; but damp stye-floors more particularly. Bricks are bad, causing cramp as much as anything, unless the pigs are so well littered up as not to come directly in contact with them. If the animals are attended to on the first appearance of cramp, no bad result need follow. Keep them dry and well bedded up, and observe the golden rule, which all should follow, with cramping pigs that are not ready for killing, "Make them work hard." In plain words, do not let the pig feed to repletion and then lie still, but keep it short of food, so that it has to worry about. Let it out into a meadow or yard, and give about half the quantity of food it would eat till the cramp disappears. In the case of an animal that is about ready for the knife, and in good condition, however, of course this would not be advisable, as it would be only taking the flesh off; but feed it on, and if it gets very bad, kill it. But the pig must be kept short and made to run about and worry, if it is not ready for killing. If this is done on the first appearance of cramp, it will soon effect a cure; but if the disease gets tight hold of the pig, and its limbs become contracted and drawn up, it may be set down as a bad job. In any case, it is a loss.

Suppose a man has one or two, or a quantity, in a stye, and they are noticed to go a little stiff. If he does not really know how to treat the disease, I guarantee he will feed the animals more tenderly and carefully than ever. They will come out and seem a little stiff, eat their usual quantity, and then lie down. In a few days, perhaps, they will get quite stiff, and as soon as they are fed will drop down in the bed. As time goes on, they will get up with great pain, the fore and hind legs will be drawn together, and their eyes protrude out of their head. They will then get gradually worse and unable to move, and be only just able to get their heads in the trough. In fact, they will be killed with kindness.

When the disease first appears, it will be after the pig has been lying still awhile; but after it has been running about a little, it will disappear. So that a lot of pigs at its commencement may be taken to market, and whilst they are kept hustled about they will appear all right, and nothing seem wrong till the next morning.

Cramp must be got rid of, then, on its first appearance, by keeping the pig well exercised and short of food. It is seldom that cramp is seen after March, and hardly ever on pigs when suckling; when they are taken from the sow is the time it often attacks them, and is then most to be feared, as the pig is of but little value for killing.

"*Stye-baked*" is when the pig gets a nasty hard-cracked hide, and it will never do any good till this is remedied. It is caused by lying in a bad place and being otherwise neglected; and when it gets thoroughly set, it will take a long time to get the pig started in a thriving way again. I should not advise anyone to purchase any in this state, even if large enough for money, as they will only be a trouble.

Measles—breaking out in spots, and having eruptions and sores—are not much to be feared so long as the pigs eat well. A little purifying opening medicine and change of food will generally alter this state of things. Giving too heating foods will often cause a breaking out. This, of course, can soon be remedied by giving more cooling foods. When pigs are doing extra well, they will often break out in spots, and they should then have a little physic occasionally.

Internal Diseases.—Pigs are liable to internal complaints, such as disease of the lungs, liver, and some parts of the bowels; and many are killed, when apparently thriving and doing well, that are badly diseased in one or other of these organs. If one pig in a stye is noticed to feed irregularly, and seems uneasy and restless, while its food does not seem to do it any good, and in spite of the best attention does not thrive, then the quicker that pig is killed the better, as it may be set down as having some of its organs in a diseased state.

Craving for Impure Foods or Drink.—Anyone who has kept a number of feeding pigs or suckling sows has no doubt found them chew the dung in the stye or yard and seemingly suck out the moisture, or go to the drainings of the stye, or a dirty pool in the farmyard, and drink the muck there. When a pig has this morbid and unhealthy appetite, it shows that the stomach is wrong and that the digestive organs are out of order. This is caused by heating foods and those that may contain impure ingredients in them; or in the case of a suckling sow, by being pulled down low and weak, so that she cannot digest her food properly. When this is noticed in any case, it must be stopped. If the foods are hot, change them. Give a good cleansing, purifying physic—in bad cases, cattle salts. Then give an admixture of sulphur, madder, and other ingredients that act on the stomach and blood, and make them throw out any impurities they may be absorbing in the system; for it stands to reason that a pig eating filth must be harbouring disease in its system. Give plenty of green food and also earth, and if it can be done, let them out in a meadow or field, so that they get back their normal healthy appetite. There is no doubt but that swine fever is fostered by such a state as this, if allowed to continue.

A Common-sense Practical Criticism of the Present Method of Exterminating Swine Fever. — When the Swine Fever Commission sat to take evidence, practical men pointed out their belief in confining the restrictions on movement to the infected or suspected places *only*. That was my idea, and I said so before the Commission. If the Board of Agriculture had at the first taken this advice, if they had made a code of rules, and heavily punished anyone who moved suspected or diseased pigs, or animals that had been in contact with them (the moving of such pigs could be entirely stopped by proper management), and if they had stamped it out and prevented it from spreading where it broke out and was reported, then there would have been no need for local authorities to prohibit transit from one district to another, nor of such things as "infected areas" or "zones," &c. I should like members of local and other authorities, and all interested, to follow me closely here, as I am giving the opinion of all practical pig-keepers who have been severe sufferers through these "areas," &c., and the prohibition of whole counties or districts one from another.

Before going further, I would touch on one point. Many inexperienced people say: "Why does not each district breed its own pigs, and not have them from another district?" My reply to this is that in some districts (mostly agricultural), pig-keepers find they pay best to breed and sell as stores, or from the teat. Others find it answer best to buy to feed, such as men in manufacturing districts, waste-consumers, dairymen, &c.; and one person is as glad to get customers for his surplus pigs as others are to buy. One district gets a little overdone, and another gets a shorter supply than is needed. Note, especially, the last four years in this respect—the rushing of buyers after feeding pigs at one time and in some places, while at another time districts were glutted, and there was a difficulty in finding buyers. When this free buying and selling is stopped, it is a serious injury to both districts. In 1892 eight-weeks-old pigs were worth 4s. a head less in Beds than in Herts, because of restrictions; and yet the animals in the former county were often miles from diseased places. Again, one district does not consume, or require for killing, half the hogs it fats, while in other localities there is a demand for the surplus. It will thus be seen that stopping the transit from one place to another is more serious than many imagine; in fact, it is often disastrous to the small working pig-keeper, whose little capital is perhaps wholly absorbed in his pigs.

Districts and counties have regulations framed against one another, and their boundaries run into one another, so that pigs may be perfectly healthy at one farm, and near no disease, yet one person cannot buy of a neighbour half-a-mile off, because he would have to take the animals across certain roads. When certain counties make regulations against, and restrict movement from, other counties at a distance, people do not know where it is safe to buy and where it is not. How should they? I might give a few instances of how foolishly such rules work, but space forbids. I may, however, say that, had I been so inclined, I could have lawfully moved pigs to distant districts from within a hundred yards or less of an infected or suspected place; yet the same authority's order that permitted this, prevented me from sending them from a healthy stye, *and with no disease within twenty miles!* This is a fair sample of how one local authority's order against another works.

If the Board of Agriculture would take practical steps to prevent people from moving diseased and suspected pigs, and stamp out all cases promptly, or strictly isolate all pigs whilst under investigation, then all this power of one local authority making orders and prohibition against the pigs of another district would be unnecessary. I think all thoughtful members of local authorities will agree with me in this; in fact, I see no room for argument against it—it is so clear. But till proper rules are framed, and detectives appointed, diseased pigs will continue to be taken from one place to another. It is no more unsafe to move pigs two hundred miles than to send them two miles, if all be done as I suggest. Have counties that have for years totally prohibited, or imposed severe restrictions on, outside pigs—such as Staffordshire, Worcestershire, and Shropshire, &c.—secured any immunity from disease at the present time? It is proved that they have not. This, therefore, shows that local powers, imposing restrictions against others whilst they have disease themselves, simply inflict an injury on pig-keepers and trade, and do no good; therefore, such power should be taken from them by the Board of Agriculture, not in an arbitrary, but in a friendly way. Instead of these diversified, perplexing, and unmeaning local orders, the Board of Agriculture should ask all local authorities to help in carrying out one practical code of rules and regulations all over Great Britain and Ireland alike. If in twelve months' time this does not decrease swine fever, I shall be convinced that it arises otherwise than through the germs from diseased pigs.

I am not surprised at no good having been done as yet when I know how suspected and diseased pigs are still smuggled about, and the many ways in which the germs may easily be carried about, and no real means taken to stop it. When the Swine Fever Bill was made law, I welcomed it, as I hoped this smuggling about would be stopped, and swine fever exterminated; but directly I saw there were to be no hard-and-fast rules to go by, and that it was based on experimental and theoretical ideas, I prophesied failure; and I do so now (in spite of a temporary lull in reported cases) until a totally different system is adopted, even though the Government may spend the ratepayers' and the taxpayers' money, to the enormous extent they have been doing during the last few years, for twenty years longer. Why should this smuggling about and want of proper precaution in stamping out reported cases ruin careful trade and movement of undeniably healthy pigs? It is the case, however, and that makes me indignant.

The loss to pig-keepers through having to buy and sell to disadvantage because of trade being stopped by the restrictions, the unnecessary trouble and expense involved in getting movement licenses, and the bad prices obtained—many being unable to make anything like fair value—has discouraged so many that they have, and are, giving over keeping pigs. If space permitted, I should have liked to give for consideration a code of drastic rules and regulations to exterminate swine fever from the country.

I am convinced that closing the sales against store pigs, and causing all fat hogs to be sent straight to where they are to be killed; detection of, and information regarding, sickly pigs; and isolation, and disinfection, would be steps in the right direction. Rather, however, than go against the wishes of many, I say, Make it impossible for any but healthy pigs from yards where all are healthy to go to the sales which have been the hotbeds and disseminators of disease in the past through these known and unsound pigs being cleared off there. Further on, I give some hints on stopping the movement of suspected or infected pigs, isolation, stamping out, &c. There need be no restrictions on moving healthy pigs where there is no disease. Anyone could move such with safety if a proper workable code of regulations were made as I suggest, and of which I give a brief outline further on. If I appear to repeat myself, it is simply due to an earnest endeavour to convince my readers as to the soundness of my argument, to show why the extermination of swine fever has been a failure up to now, and to indicate how sound remedial measures might be adopted.

The Causes of Illness and Deaths that are often mistaken for Swine Fever.—Pigs are considered by many as hardy animals, but illness and deaths are easily brought about and in various ways. Changing the diet very suddenly, especially in the case of pigs that have been kept short and on inferior feed, and are then bought by a feeder and fed to repletion on richer food, or even food of no better quality but quite different, will often cause illness. I have seen numbers of them that have died through this only, and yet have been condemned as having had swine fever. Buyers of strange pigs should always feed sparingly at first, and give a little physic occasionally.

Pigs that have been shut up in a close place, and kept in during the day, will, if let out in the hot sun, or the damp and cold, often sicken and die, being afterwards condemned as having had swine fever. Carting of such pigs to market, and the consequent exposure, will often sicken and kill them: this also is "diagnosed" as swine fever. Feeding pigs to repletion on liquid food, and carting them about, is sure to hurt them, and invariably makes them sick. I have had fat hogs and stores, perfectly healthy and doing well, which, when moved with a bellyful of food, have been killed thereby, especially in hot, sultry weather, and often before they have been an hour in the cart. I therefore advise anyone to drive, cart, or move pigs on an *empty stomach.* If anything is given the same day, it should be dry corn and water only. Many pigs have weak hearts, and there is danger in moving them about. This and sheer fright have made them reel and stagger, and sometimes die. Fat sows, in hot weather especially, should be well fasted before they are carted about. I have had these die in being moved.

I would advise people to note these instructions when moving pigs, and when buying fresh ones. I would also draw the attention of the swine fever officials to this matter, and ask them not so hastily to condemn freshly-moved pigs as having swine fever. Pigs that have been kept in a warm-littered place till reared have often been bought by dealers, taken to market, and laid for hours on a bare paved pen floor; perhaps it has been pouring with rain, or there have been a cutting wind and sleet. They have then been taken away, and some have sickened and died quickly afterwards. The "vet." has been called in, and another case of swine fever declared: result, dealer humbugged, fresh restrictions on the county imposed, and trade stopped, *all through one error.* Again, pigs that have been sent from the sows and a good, warm, well-littered stye, where straw is plentiful, are bought by a man who puts them on a bare brick or sawdusted floor. Perhaps, originally, they were fed on everything of the best—milk-good meals, or middlings. Their new owner gives them house, wash, turnips, or bran, and they sicken and die. "Vet." is called in: swine fever (?) again. An innocent man is interviewed, or threatened and bullied, and, unjustly and at serious loss, has his premises closed for months.

I am not going to defend the dealers as an immaculate class, as I know there are plenty with such a conscience that, *whilst knowing the risk*, they will buy a lot of doubtful pigs at half their proper value, not considering what others stand the chance to suffer so long as they have a good haul.

How Swine Fever is Spread and Trade Stopped.—The genuine Bedfordshire trade—and the trade and pig-keeping in England generally—has been seriously injured by buying risky pigs, not only in Bedfordshire, but from numerous other counties—in fact, in any pig-breeding or feeding districts in England and no doubt in Ireland. Careful feeders and dealers refuse to buy such stock at any price to take to their healthy yards or send to others. Others not so particular will run the risk at half price. I am, of course, now referring to the pigs "stuffed" in auction sales, the owners of which know well that they are not right. The animals look what is termed "dickey"; nobody knows where they come from; suspicion is aroused; there is a whispering round the ring as they come in with hanging heads and tails, and perhaps there is a cough. The pigs are run round the ring. Bids are slow, too; but at last some speculator says 5s.; another bids 5s. 6d.; and by sixpenny bids they get to 8s. Down goes the hammer. Then there is a discussion. Pigs big enough to make 16s. are sold for 8s.! A man is going to get 8s. per pig, or lose 8s., or cause someone else to not only lose perhaps 16s., but get his stock and yard tainted. Not only this: but how about the quantity of healthy smart pigs that go in the same ring, and may actually lie with their noses close to these "doubtfuls" for hours? They may have swine fever, or they may not. "Veterinary inspectors are appointed," many may say, "to condemn fever-infected pigs in the market and sales, and have them confiscated and buried, and the senders heavily punished." The inspectors may only *suspect* any of these so-called "dickey" pigs, and so are still helpless, as they cannot condemn or kill on mere suspicion. Perhaps these pigs are bought and sent hundreds of miles off, and a good haul made. Perhaps they are put in the same trucks as undeniably healthy ones, and may, one way or another, mix with hundreds more. They *may not* have swine fever, but then they *may*. If the latter be the case, how about the others in that sale or market? and how about those that may come into contact with them directly or indirectly? Such pigs as these have in years gone by passed through a good many hands, and through a good many sales. A buyer gets "bitten." He afterwards sees the pigs have something serious the matter with them. He has bought them with all faults, and thinks it nothing amiss to do as he was done by.

Several instances of diseased pigs being found in certain public markets or sales have been noted in the papers lately, and all of the pigs have been detained for days. In one instance a man sent some diseased pigs to a market two consecutive weeks: the pigs were killed, *the buyer was compensated*, and no further inquiry was made about the sender! Here is a case for those who talk about drastic remedies and restrictions! Compare it with that of the man who *innocently* breaks an order *in moving healthy pigs*, and is mulcted in about £20, as I was once. But in all these cases we hear of no punishment! It should have been *hard labour* in the case I have quoted. Theorists, who talk of restrictions over large areas *against healthy pigs*, should read this and understand it; they will thus see how disease is spread, and that it is not done by healthy pigs from healthy yards.

Why should not a system be worked out to make it impossible to send such pigs to the sales at all without detection and heavy punishment? It could be done easily. Why should genuine trade between large breeding and feeding districts be stopped because of this? Why should not undeniably healthy pigs—stores or fat—be moved straight from healthy yards to other healthy yards anywhere, or bought through the sales or markets? The former has in the past been the only safe way to buy and sell, but both ways can be made safe with a little energy. We want a thorough system to stop fraudulent practices entirely by making them impossible without detection and heavy punishment. Neither the authorities nor private persons can do this by themselves. Combination of both, and the removal of foolish restrictions, can quickly put things right.

Swine Fever and its Results—How to Stamp it out Quickly and Economically.—This dreaded disease is supposed to have been introduced into England about thirty years or more ago. Previous to that time pigs were liable to different kinds of illnesses—not contagious—by which they were attacked in a similar way to swine fever; and, as is the case to-day, no doubt one disease was mistaken for another till it was seen how contagious the imported disease was, and what heavy losses it entailed. I have heard old pig-keepers talk about "garget" in pigs, and the heavy losses caused thereby. This was due to indigestible foods, such as too many acorns (especially green ones), new damp corn given too liberally, &c.; and the same thing occurs to-day, but it is often mistaken for swine fever by the veterinaries.

When I wrote the First Edition of this book, some years ago, I, like the majority of pig-keepers, was under the impression that swine fever could be brought on by bad foods, bad smells, insanitary places, colds, neglect, and so on. The veterinary authorities, however, say that sickness and death may be brought on by these things, but not real swine fever; that it is impossible for pigs to take the latter except from a diseased pig, directly or indirectly; and that it is spread by means of minute germs or eggs that pass from infected pigs with the urine or droppings, or with the breath, and by some means are picked up by others. Having no reason to doubt this, I will take it for granted that it is the case, and will ask all thoughtful readers to look at it in this light with a view to ascertaining how it can be exterminated from Great Britain. Viewed from this standpoint, it appears easy to get rid of the disease by killing all pigs that fall with it and are on the same premises, directly it is without doubt found to be swine fever, and then thoroughly disinfecting the premises and so *killing all the germs*, taking strict precautions in the meantime that no germs can be taken off the same premises to contaminate others. My idea of the way to do this I will try to give further on.

The Symptoms and Nature of Swine Fever make it difficult for anyone to determine by outside appearance whether the case is one of swine fever or not, in the first stages. That the post-mortem examinations of the bowels are thoroughly unreliable (at any rate when a pig first falls or dies suddenly), is proved by the great mistakes made, by the fact that clever veterinary surgeons in most animal complaints cannot agree, and by the fact that a few pigs have died, been examined, and pronounced fever-stricken, while others that they had lain with never ailed. Cases of sows dying whilst pigs were sucking them have been pronounced by the present veterinary experts in London to be swine fever, yet the sucking pigs have actually never ailed, but have thriven and done well. Instances like these prove that post-mortems by London experts are not to be implicitly depended upon.

I believe this disease has not been studied enough by the profession. It has not been to their advantage to do so, for who would call in a professional man to doctor a sick pig? The attendance, &c., would cost more than the value of a pig if cured. One had better let it take its chance or kill it. Therefore, I hope the profession will not be offended, as I only give the opinion of pig-keepers generally. I may, however, say one thing. The London experts either mean right, and think they can tell, or it is guesswork, in which case they should be honest and own that they cannot determine the case with certainty by the entrails received, especially some days after death in hot weather. Whole yards have been cleared of healthy invaluable breeding sows and pigs, when only a pig or two have died of some other of the numerous sicknesses all pigs are liable to, and it has become quite a byword with practical pig-keepers, and many experienced veterinaries, that not one-fourth of the condemned pigs have had swine fever at all.

The Ill-effects of Adulterated Foods.—Before killing a pig, where any are reported ill or dying, a sample and particulars of the food should be taken and sent to London to be analysed, or identified and described, and it should be noted how the pigs have been bedded and housed. If this is carefully done the cause of a lot of illness and deaths would be easily discovered. Being in the trade as a seller of pig-foods, I have often had sent to me from shippers samples of the veriest rubbish, offered at a low price—often nothing but chafings of foreign corn, small seeds, and dust dressed up, with not one particle of goodness in it. Vendors of pig-foods dare not offer or sell this stuff as it is, as people with any knowledge would see what it was; but it is bought and mixed in small proportions with otherwise good foods, as middlings, &c., so carefully, that it would puzzle many to know such stuff was put in it. The vendor gets a double profit, or cuts under his simpler or more conscientious rival. It often gets overdone, and pigs begin to do badly; sometimes they are taken ill and die, and it is then stated that they have had swine fever.

I would bring this to the notice of the Board of Agriculture and Board of Trade, and ask why the working of the Adulteration of Feeding Stuffs, &c., Act is so inoperative. Pure middlings are the safest and best possible food for pigs, yet so common is the practice of millers and dealers to put all the rubbish, dust, chafings, and seeds from their foreign corn in with them, that a stoppage of this by getting at the *mixer* for selling middlings, &c., adulterated, and heavy punishment, would deter others. If, however, any move is made to make this Act operative on feeding stuffs, as I suggest, I trust that the man to be punished will be the one who puts the impurities in, and not the retailer who unwittingly buys it as pure, and might be found selling it. If the latter can prove he bought it as pure, let the punishment fall on the mixer.

Real (Typhoid) Swine Fever is dreadfully contagious. If there were say ten sows and a hundred youngish pigs in a yard freely mixed together, and swine fever broke out, it would in time clear the lot, except, perhaps, a few sows and stores of strong constitution; but it is very seldom that many escape, especially tender pigs and those that are kept warm and well fed. Fever can also be easily taken from infected pigs to healthy ones by persons going direct from one place to another, even a hundred miles off.

The post-mortem examination having proved to be a failure, I advise, instead of the ruthless slaughter of whole yards of healthy pigs in mistake, the adoption of other means, namely, *isolation and disinfection.* When pigs begin to fall with any illness suspected to be swine fever, or other sickness, as I have mentioned, they quickly go off their feed. Directly any pigs do this, and do not come out as usual when food is put in, or if turned out go about with hanging head and tail, and appear lifeless and listless, they should be removed to an isolated place, and one person appointed to attend them. He should not go near where other pigs are, or where others are likely to go. The attendant should throw plenty of disinfectant about and round the places, especially if others appear dull, and the owner has strong suspicion it is swine fever. The animals should also be kept a little short of food. It should be judged whether the usual food or anything else may not have caused the mischief. A little powdered madder and sulphur—or, if a stubborn case of costiveness, some salts—may put them right. They might have been overfed, or have had some rubbish in the food, and sickened; at any rate, in a few days or a week, if treated so, they will be all right and feeding well, or will be getting worse. One or two may die: but that will not prove that swine fever is the cause. When a pig has the fever advanced, it will eat hardly anything, but has a craving for drink. It scours and smells badly, will creep out of the way, and, as the disease progresses, will fall off in flesh, perhaps cough, and be sick at times. In the later stages it may be costive, and turn red on the skin. I do not believe in pigs being condemned that were healthy and feeding, taken ill, and dead in a few days. Fever comes on gradually, by stages, almost imperceptibly, except to a man who feeds pigs regularly, and who quickly notes anything amiss.

When it is decided that the case is swine fever, all the pigs that have come into contact, as well as the affected ones, should be killed. For those affected, and which do not feed *before* the police are called in, one-half the value is plenty; in fact, they are not worth twopence to the owner. But for all that fall after, and for those which feed all right till killed, the owner should be paid the full value as if healthy; thus, we should prevent unprincipled men from killing the few that are bad, and burying them, while sending all the apparently healthy ones off to a sale. Those which are feeding and doing well should be killed and dressed on the premises, and sold, if found clear.

With *strict isolation, thorough disinfection, and other proper precautions* I do not hesitate to say that it is perfectly safe to keep suspected pigs in a stye or buildings twenty yards from healthy ones, till one can ascertain whether swine fever is present or not. But if, for a week or two after all are slaughtered, any in the near vicinity (say fifty yards off) are not allowed to be moved (unless the owner has fat ones, and cares to kill on the premises, and take the carcases from there), this could not reasonably be objected to by any owner. As for indiscriminately stopping the sale of healthy pigs miles from a case like this, or even at the other end of the parish, it is all nonsense, if the precautions I have mentioned are taken.

Results Attained by the Old Administrative Bodies.—Up to November 1st, 1893, no real practical measures were taken all over the country to get rid of the disease altogether. Local authorities had power to make any restrictions or regulations they thought fit to stop the spread of the disease, *except against pigs from Ireland.* They had the power to kill and pay compensation out of the local rates. Some counties spent a lot of money and were obliged to stop, beaten. After this, diseased pigs were in many parts dying off on farms for weeks without any proper precautions being taken to prevent the germs from being carried abroad, so that in the whole district and in other counties pig-keeping was made very risky.

Results Attained by the Administrative Body since November 1st, 1893.—In November 1893, the Government took the matter *partially* over; and that "partially" was a mistake. I hope before going further that the reader will understand how I look on this matter. Why the local authorities failed, and why the Government, with unlimited funds at their disposal, after spending immense sums, have completely failed to do any good towards clearing the country, as yet, may be thus summed up: First, they have *not made it impossible for anyone to move a sickly pig* (*knowing it is sickly*) without detection and heavy punishment (see p. 77); and secondly, the most *scandalous neglect has been carried on in "preventing" the disease from being spread after cases of suspicion have been reported.* Here is the cause of failure in a nutshell. Pigs have actually been carted about through villages, and miles along high roads to towns, *direct from amongst other pigs that have been condemned* as having swine fever, to see if they have got it! Thus, what with the excrement, urine, and litter droppings from the cart, and the litter blown about, the risk to any pigs that came along those roads, or were lying alongside them, can be understood. Suspected animals have even been taken to places where other pigs were, to be killed, in order to see whether diseased or not!

When cases have been reported no proper isolation has been made imperative, or other precaution taken. One suspected case in my own village (two years ago) was reported, whereupon everybody around wanted to see the suspects and maul them about, and then could go amongst their own pigs or anyone else's if they liked. It was not swine fever: but if it had been, what then? Yet at the same time pig-yards that were nowhere near (like my own) were closed *for weeks after it was proved not to be swine fever.* In another case a sow suckling some pigs, and two other pigs—large stores—were taken suddenly ill, and one, I think, died before the owner could report. The vet. came *after a day or two*, the others dying in the meantime. The owner got not a penny compensation, and had his places closed. The dead pigs and sow were condemned on the post-mortem system, and a man was appointed to bury them. Half-drunk, he smothered himself with blood, stabbing and rolling on the pigs. A pretence was made to disinfect himself by washing his hands and shoes. Actually, during the time he was attending the pigs, and after he had buried them, he was allowed to go where he liked, and in my absence I was told he was on my premises with the same clothes on smothered with blood. I might, had I not known where he had been, have had him to help me move large quantities of healthy ones. The sequel was, though condemned, the case was proved to be *not* swine fever, for the owner was naturally annoyed by the treatment he had received, and would not have the other pigs killed. The sow that died suddenly was condemned as having swine fever; she left a litter of healthy young pigs that never did ail, though sucking to the last and after she died! I know by experience that if it had been swine fever they would have fallen directly, and so would all in the styes adjoining, unless saved by a miracle.

Another case that came under my notice: Some pigs died at a farm. After investigation the rest were all killed, yet I am perfectly satisfied they had not swine fever. Still, it did a great deal of injury in the neighbourhood. In slaughtering them, however, the blood was washed into a public watercourse that ran through another farm-yard and down a village where other pig-keepers got water to feed their pigs. I mention these cases as instances of how suspected cases have been continually treated, and as illustrating the gross carelessness *and lack of means to prevent the spread of the infection.* Can we wonder at real cases of swine fever being spread after having been reported (rather than *stamped* out) by the officials in charge?

Treatment of English and Irish Pig-keepers.—Pigs in Bedfordshire and other parts could not be moved at all from healthy places where bred *miles from disease*, and in other cases only at great expense; whilst in some districts they could be moved from yards close to infected places. At the same time pigs could, until November, 1895, be sent from tainted districts in Ireland to any place in England, and the authorities were helpless to prevent their coming. No inquiry, it seems, was made as to where these Irish pigs came from, nor was any licence required. This was carried on for twelve months! I will not further comment on it, but as a business man will simply ask whether those who have the making of the orders are fit for such an important position.

How to get rid of Swine Fever.—The way to exterminate swine fever is to get all to report as soon as they have pigs with anything suspicious about them, and to prevent anyone from moving suspected animals off his premises. This can only be done by having one central administrative office, say in London, conducted by a committee of *experienced* men, to receive reports, &c.

The first thing the officials should do would be to have circulars printed and circulated, showing all pig-keepers, and anyone interested, the nature of swine fever, and pointing out also the fact that it cannot be produced spontaneously: they would thus convince and gain the help and co-operation of all pig-keepers, auctioneers, dealers, the police, local inspectors and authorities, and butchers, and it could be got rid of in a short time. Only sensible and practical restrictions would be imposed, and these should secure hearty co-operation. Without the help and approval of the above classes it will be hard work to do any good. In this matter the Board have made a great mistake. They made a muddling set of rules to start with, gave pig-keepers any amount of useless trouble to get licences, &c., stopped the buying and selling of healthy pigs, and took no proper precautions to stamp swine fever out where reported. By stopping trade they have caused serious loss—often 20s. or 30s. on a litter of pigs, and 10s. or more on fat hogs—and then have said it could not be helped, and asked for the assistance of all pig-keepers, with the natural result that they are in bad odour with all who were anxious to help.

One set of rules should be made for the whole of Great Britain *and Ireland;* or if Ireland is not included, and under the same treatment, then pigs should be precluded from being sent from Ireland alive whilst disease exists there. A code of rules should be made to work automatically. Copies of them should be placed in the hands of all the police; they would then know what to do in case an outbreak were reported to them, and should see these rules strictly carried out. Anyone should also be able to get copies from the police gratis. Wilful infringement of the rules should make anyone liable to heavy punishment. A duly qualified veterinary inspector should be appointed for every borough which has a jurisdiction to itself, and also for every petty sessional division —not necessarily one for each, as one could take all, or part, of a county and the boroughs in it. Directly a suspected case is reported to the police, their duty should be to fetch or send for the appointed inspector. The policeman should report particulars on proper forms to his superintendent, and he to the central office, or the constable direct to both, with the inspector's opinion as well. The constable should ascertain from the owner if the affected pigs, or any others, have been brought on to the premises lately; if so, where from; and should wire, write, or see (if handy) the police superintendent of that division. If in his own police division, but some distance off, he should write or wire to the police stationed there. Thorough enquiries should be made there, but no action taken unless the pigs fall ill at once on removal, or any sick pigs are on the premises, or any other suspicious circumstances arise, when he should have power to fetch the vet. Still, there should be no tyrannical shutting up of a man's place for months where he has nothing but healthy pigs, and has had no disease on or near his yards for months before.

If prompt isolation were effected, and a thorough investigation made at once, smuggling diseased pigs as it is now done would be stopped.

Rules to Prevent Suspected Pigs from being Sent to Auction Sales.—No one who has thoroughly healthy pigs to sell would mind seeing his name above the pens, together with information as to where the animals came from. Breeders of good-class stock, indeed, would, I think, welcome this rule. Well, let this information be put in plain letters over the pens, on a card or something, by a policeman or other official, and remain there until removed with the pigs by the buyer. This practice would not injure trade or be any inconvenience, except to the man who might try to get suspected pigs off his hands.

If any pigs in the markets or sales, on examination by the inspector, appear sickly and very suspicious, he should ascertain all he can about them. He should have power to isolate them for a day or two. If they feed and do all right the next day, they should be allowed to be moved, and the owner recompensed for any loss. If it can be proved that the pigs will not feed properly, and were really ill before they were sent from the owner's yard, or any pig was moved thence while unwell, or they were sent away because others on the premises were so, then that man has no excuse against heavy punishment (see page 78). I would, however, ask readers now to refer to my remarks on pages 75 and 76 about sickness and deaths caused through moving, fresh food, &c.

If such rules were made, and a system organised for the *whole* of Great Britain and worked by the police, diversified local orders being done away with, swine fever could be got rid of at little cost, quickly, and with but little hindrance to trade.

It is sometimes stated that swine fever is more difficult to deal with than cattle diseases. I think the reverse, as cattle, sheep, &c., roam over a large area in the summer, and many pass along the roads; further, they may get at one another over the hedges, before it can be ascertained that anything is wrong. Pigs, however, are as a rule confined in styes or yards, and the disease can easily be stamped out in small compass.

One more important matter. Let it be thoroughly understood between the head office, the police, and pig-keepers, that all information given by pig-keepers will be regarded as confidential. Although persons who have not moved anything wrong are naturally anxious for a thorough investigation, yet as business men they expect their private business affairs to be kept private. Neither do they care to be bullied into giving information about any part of their private business by travelling inspectors, while insulting threats naturally will not gain the help necessary. The police, with a little help, through their network of connections, and through being on the spot daily, would be able to carry out the regulations more cheaply and effectually than any other officials. Daily attendance on the spot is required, and I cannot see the utility of appointing so many travelling inspectors of no experience at high salaries, and who have no notion of valuing pigs: they sometimes award double the cost of the animals, and at others abuse pig-keepers who refuse to take less than fair value.

A Few Words about Bedfordshire-bred Pigs.—Bedfordshire is reckoned a risky place to buy from. This is all wrong. If cases of genuine swine fever were properly investigated where pigs that went away from Bedfordshire fell with it, it would be found that they were bought at the auctions not only in Bedfordshire, but in the counties adjoining, as well as in the Midland and Eastern counties, or were pigs that had been in the same places or mixed with auction pigs. Where the disease occurred in freshly-moved pigs, it could be proved to be through the rubbish sent to the sales in most cases; and although it can be proved that not one case of disease was sent from Bedfordshire in 1894, yet the Government travellers at that time were doing their utmost to get distant local authorities to boycott Bedfordshire-bred pigs, saying it was unsafe to allow them to come in. I myself have sent large quantities weekly from healthy styes in Bedfordshire during the last two years, and all were perfectly sound. Not one lot fell with fever out of the thousands I sent by rail. This is a plain fact that cannot be controverted, and is the best argument I can bring forward to prove that no restrictions whatever are necessary against sending pigs from one locality to another, so long as they are not mixed up with suspected pigs sent knowingly to the sales; and that if disease does exist in a county, healthy pigs from healthy yards could be moved out with safety, provided they do not and have not come into direct, or indirect, contact with diseased ones, or with those from premises adjoining unhealthy yards. All local orders as to "areas," "zones," &c., should be done away with, and restrictions imposed only on the suspected or infected places, and a few hundred yards around. The disease must, of course, be strictly isolated and not allowed to spread. The man who would move suspected or diseased pigs must be—and he can be—stopped or given a long term of imprisonment.

Conclusion.—In the present edition I have devoted a good deal of space to showing how pig-keeping is seriously injured and handicapped, and trade stopped, by restrictions on sales, and how this could be altered before the industry suffers further. I should have liked to go further into details, and give a code of regulations which in my idea would attain that object, but space forbids. I would also again remind my readers of the necessity of breeding good stock, and should like to see County Councillors and managers of local shows, &c., devote a little more time and attention to pig-keeping by giving a little advice on the pig from a sanitary and humane point of view. Great cruelty is ignorantly practised on pigs in the way they are kept, fed, and housed. It shocks the public mind when horses or cattle are turned out in a field and half-starved. People, however, little know how many pigs die of starvation and neglect!

Considering the great usefulness of the pig and its real necessity as a waste-consumer, turning into good bacon what no other animal will eat, its effects in fertilising the large and the small cultivator's land, I say again that the pig is much neglected in this country. Let us hope better days are in store for such an important contributor to our food supply.

Hints on Seeing that Pigs are Healthy when Purchasing.—I cannot conclude without making a few more remarks on what the buyer of swine should do. As I stated before, buy some to come straight from the place where bred, if possible. See that they are good feeders, and that they are bright on the skin. Old hardy stores in poor condition will, of course, have a rough hide, but it should not be hide-bound, or stye-baked, or scurfy. Their eyes should be bright and wide open; their tails should be well twisted; and if they stretch and rub themselves well against anything they may come in contact with, it is a good sign that they are in a thriving condition. If they appear dull and listless, go about with drooping heads, and huddle themselves in a heap when let out of a stye to have a run, then they are not in sound condition.

In the cold weather a young pig will naturally crouch and shiver when exposed to the weather, and will want to get back to its bed; but if they appear this way inclined in the summer, and want to creep into the straw, they should be avoided. A man with a practised eye can quickly see if they are thriving and doing well in a farmyard or breeder's stye, but when they are carted and moved about, it is more difficult. In buying any in a stye, it is well to let them out in a yard to have a run; anyone can then see if they are about straight. During the winter months of the year, when the cramp is prevalent, it can then be seen if they are quite free from this.

When cramp is on them they usually look rather dull and dirty about the eye and face.

Evils of Dirty Styes.—Uncleanliness in the stye and yard should always be avoided by those who wish to keep their pigs in a healthy condition. The animals should never be allowed to stand up to their hocks in muck to eat their food, nor to lie in it. A pig feeling inclined to go and wallow in the mud-heap, or in a dirty ditch, is another affair altogether, and so long as he carries out his natural inclination there is not much harm to fear. But when he is penned up in a dirty wet stye day after day, and perhaps around the trough all is dung and muck, he will first put his foot in the muck and then into the food, and will actually have to consume a quantity of this muck, which looks more like breeding disease than not.

On many farms a lot of pigs are fattened in a stye, or a sow farrows in a stye and brings up a lot of pigs; as soon as they are ready to move, the stye is cleansed out and a bundle of litter is put in, and another lot of pigs are placed there at once, or a sow is put in to pig there. This is done time after time, perhaps from one year's end to another; or, if the stye lies empty for a time, it is unintentionally so, or perhaps it remains in the state it was in when the last lot were removed, till it is found to be wanted, and is then cleaned out, and some more pigs put in at once. It stands to reason that that stye has had no chance to get purified, and that there will be bad stale smells in the floor and walls, which cannot be good for the pigs, even if it does not actually cause disease. Every time a stye is emptied it should be thoroughly cleaned and scraped out, walls well lime-washed, some loose lime thrown all over the floor, and the place left open so that the wind and air can get in for a week or more. This would cost but a trifle, and the pigs would be much better than if put into a tainted stye. Such an affair as this is thought to be of little significance by many pig-keepers, but I consider it to be of the utmost importance.

APPENDIX.

WHILST correcting the proofs of this edition (December 5th) I received a letter from a correspondent, in which he said: "We are very much hampered here with the Swine Fever Regulations. I live in Sussex, but close on Hampshire. Our market town is Petersfield, in Hampshire, but our Sussex authorities will not allow a pig to be brought from Hampshire into Sussex. *The consequence is we are obliged to sell our pigs at any price.*"

This is only one specimen of what I receive from all parts of England, as well as from my own neighbourhood. Shillington—in and around which is a large pig-breeding and feeding district—is in Beds.; the market town is Hitchin, Herts., about five miles distant; yet a fat hog cannot be taken from Shillington to Hitchin. This is not because any disease exists at Shillington; in fact, there is no reason whatever. It is a matter of the authorities in one county making a restriction against another because they must do something, little considering the hardship they are causing so needlessly.

The authorities of Derbyshire and Staffordshire—counties that find it pay better to feed than to breed, and are large buyers—prohibit pigs from a large area, comprising a group of counties. They, however, have a motive: they have had a lot of disease sent from that group through sale pigs. Yet this indiscriminate prohibition is a serious injury to their buyers, and to those who have healthy pigs to sell in that group. No doubt if the authorities knew they would have only undeniably healthy pigs sent in, they would relax their order. They cannot tell where it is safe and where it is not, so make a general order against all. To do away with this hardship lies with the Government: they should prevent diseased pigs from going to the sales *and being sent out.* Neither of these two counties has ever had diseased pigs consigned from any station in South Beds., yet breeders in South Beds., and buyers in Derbyshire and Staffordshire, are great sufferers in not being able to buy or sell to the best advantage because of diseased or unsound pigs having been picked up at the sales, or sound pigs having come into contact with bad ones, and gone into the latter two counties.

If all the country were thrown open to Bedfordshire pigs, and it were made impossible to send any out but what were healthy, that county would soon regain its position as a large breeding and feeding district; and, though trade might be bad at times, yet there would be an outlet somewhere at something like reasonable prices. Trade would have been bad in the county the last two years, as the country has been overdone, but these things find their level. Still, there would not have been the severe sacrifices with England an open market. "It is an ill wind that blows no one good." In this case, the fact of our pig-keepers being handicapped in their sale, and discouraged from keeping pigs, has no doubt been to the great advantage of the Continental and other foreign bacon-curing countries, and there will be yearly more foreign and less English bacon consumed whilst these indiscriminate restrictions on selling store and fat pigs exist.

I only mention the above-named counties as instances to show my point, Bedfordshire being a large breeding and feeding and the others large buying districts of fat and store pigs. I must not be mistaken as claiming special privileges for any district, but plead for an unrestricted sale of healthy pigs from any place where there is no disease or risk.

INDEX.

Catalogue of Practical Handbooks Published by L. Upcott Gill, 170, Strand, London, W.C.

American Dainties, and How to Prepare Them. By an AMERICAN LADY *In paper, price* 1s., *by post* 1s. 2d.

Angler, Book of the All-Round. A Comprehensive Treatise on Angling in both Fresh and Salt Water. In Four Divisions as named below. By JOHN BICKERDYKE. With over 220 Engravings. *In cloth, price* 5s. 6d., *by post* 5s. 10d. (A few copies of a LARGE PAPER EDITION, *bound in Roxburghe, price* 25s. *nett.*)

Angling for Coarse Fish. Bottom Fishing, according to the Methods in use on the Thames, Trent, Norfolk Broads, and elsewhere. Illustrated. *In paper, price* 1s., *by post* 1s. 2d.

Angling for Pike. The most approved Methods of Fishing for Pike or Jack. Profusely Illustrated. *In paper, price* 1s., *by post* 1s. 2d.; *cloth,* 2s. *(uncut), by post* 2s. 3d.

Angling for Game Fish. The Various Methods of Fishing for Salmon; Moorland, Chalk-stream, and Thames Trout; Grayling and Char. Well Illustrated. *In paper, price* 1s. 6d., *by post* 1s. 9d.

Angling in Salt Water. Sea Fishing with Rod and Line, from the Shore, Piers, Jetties, Rocks, and from Boats; together with Some Account of Hand-Lining. Over 50 Engravings. *In paper, price* 1s., *by post,* 1s. 2d.; *cloth,* 2s. *(uncut), by post* 2s. 3d.

Aquaria, Book of. A Practical Guide to the Construction, Arrangement, and Management of Freshwater and Marine Aquaria; containing Full Information as to the Plants, Weeds, Fish, Molluscs, Insects, &c., How and Where to Obtain Them, and How to Keep Them in Health. Illustrated. By REV. GREGORY C. BATEMAN, A.K.C., and REGINALD A. R. BENNETT, B.A. *In cloth gilt, price* 5s. 6d., *by post* 5s. 10d.

Aquaria, Freshwater: Their Construction, Arrangement, Stocking, and Management. Fully Illustrated. By REV. G. C. BATEMAN, A.K.C. *In cloth gilt, price* 3s. 6d., *by post* 3s. 10d.

Aquaria, Marine: Their Construction, Arrangement, and Management. Fully Illustrated. By R. A. R. BENNETT, B.A. *In cloth gilt, price* 2s. 6d., *by post* 2s. 9d.

Australia, Shall I Try? A Guide to the Australian Colonies for the Emigrant Settler and Business Man. With two Illustrations. By GEORGE LACON JAMES. *In cloth gilt, price* 3s. 6d., *by post* 3s. 10d.

Autograph Collecting: A Practical Manual for Amateurs and Historical Students, containing ample information on the Selection and Arrangement of Autographs, the Detection of Forged Specimens, &c., &c., to which are added numerous Facsimiles for Study and Reference, and an extensive Valuation Table of Autographs worth Collecting. By HENRY T. SCOTT, M.D., L.R.C.P., &c. *In leatherette gilt, price* 7s. 6d. *nett, by post* 7s. 10d.

Bazaars and Fancy Fairs: Their Organization and Management. A Secretary's *Vade Mecum.* By JOHN MUIR. *In paper, price* 1s., *by post* 1s. 2d.

Bees and Bee-Keeping: Scientific and Practical. By F. R. CHESHIRE, F.L.S., F.R.M.S., Lecturer on Apiculture at South Kensington. *In two vols., cloth gilt, price* 16s., *by post* 16s. 6d.

Vol. I., Scientific. A complete Treatise on the Anatomy and Physiology of the Hive Bee. *In cloth gilt, price* 7s. 6d., *by post* 7s. 10d.

Vol. II., Practical Management of Bees. An Exhaustive Treatise on Advanced Bee Culture. *In cloth gilt, price* 8s. 6d., *by post* 8s. 11d.

Bee-Keeping, Book of. A very practical and Complete Manual on the Proper Management of Bees, especially written for Beginners and Amateurs who have but a few Hives. Fully Illustrated. By W. B. WEBSTER, First-class Expert, B.B.K.A. *In paper, price* 1s., *by post* 1 2d.; *cloth,* 1s. 6d., *by post* 1s. 8d.

Canary, The Pet. With some Instructions as to its Purchase, Diet, Toilette, Cage, and Sanitary Keeping. Illustrated. By W. H. BETTS, Hon. Treas. Cage Bird Club. *Price 5s. nett, by post 5s. 3d.*

Cane Basket Work: A Practical Manual on Weaving Useful and Fancy Baskets By ANNIE FIRTH. Illustrated. *In cloth gilt, price 1s. 6d., by post 1s. 8d.*

Card Conjuring: Being Tricks with Cards, and How to Perform Them By PROF. ELLIS STANYON. Illustrated, and in Coloured Wrapper. *Price by post 1s. 2d.*

Card Tricks, Book of, for Drawing-room and Stage Entertainments by Amateurs; with an exposure of Tricks as practised by Card Sharpers and Swindlers. Numerous Illustrations. By PROF. R. KUNARD. *In illustrated wrapper, price 2s. 6d., by post 2s. 9d.*

Carnation Culture, for Amateurs. The Culture of Carnations and Picotees of all Classes in the Open Ground and in Pots. Illustrated. By B. C. RAVENSCROFT. *In paper, price 1s., by post 1s. 2d.*

Cats, Domestic or Fancy: A Practical Treatise on their Antiquity, Domestication, Varieties, Breeding, Management, Diseases and Remedies, Exhibition and Judging. By JOHN JENNINGS. Illustrated. *In cloth, price 2s. 6d., by post 2s. 9d.*

Chrysanthemum Culture, for Amateurs and Professionals. Containing Full Directions for the Successful Cultivation of the Chrysanthemum for Exhibition and the Market. By B. C. RAVENSCROFT. New Edition. Illustrated. *In paper, price 1s., by post 1s. 2d.*

Chrysanthemum, The Show, and Its Cultivation. By C. SCOTT, of the Sheffield Chrysanthemum Society. *In paper, price 6d., by post 7d.*

Coins, a Guide to English Pattern, in Gold, Silver, Copper, and Pewter, from Edward I. to Victoria, with their Value. By the REV. G. F. CROWTHER, M.A. Illustrated. *In silver cloth, with gilt facsimiles of Coins, price 5s., by post 5s. 3d.*

Coins of Great Britain and Ireland, a Guide to the, in Gold, Silver, and Copper, from the Earliest Period to the Present Time, with their Value. By the late COLONEL W. STEWART THORBURN. Illustrated. *In cloth gilt, price 7s. 6d., by post 7s. 10d.*

Collie, The. Its History, Points, and Breeding. By HUGH DALZIEL, Illustrated with Coloured Frontispiece and Plates. *In paper, price 1s., by post 1s. 2d.; cloth, 2s., by post 2s 3d.*

Collie Stud Book. Edited by HUGH DALZIEL. *Price 3s. 6d. each, by post 3s. 9d. each.*

Vol. I., containing Pedigrees of 1308 of the best-known Dogs, traced to their most remote known ancestors; Show Record to Feb., 1890, &c.
Vol. II. Pedigrees of 795 Dogs, Show Record, &c.
Vol. III. Pedigrees of 786 Dogs, Show Record, &c.

Columbarium, Moore's. Reprinted Verbatim from the originial Edition of 1735, with a Brief Notice of the Author. By W. B. TEGETMEIER, F.Z.S. Member of the British Ornithologists' Union. *Price 1s., by post 1s. 2d.*

Conjuring, Book of Modern. A Practical Guide to Drawing-room and Stage Magic for Amateurs. By PROFESSOR R. KUNARD. Illustrated. *In illustrated wrapper, price 2s. 6d., by post 2s. 9d.*

Conjuring for Amateurs. A Practical Handbook on How to Perform a Number of Amusing Tricks. By PROF. ELLIS STANYON. *In paper, price 1s., by post 1s. 2d.*

Cookery, The Encyclopædia of Practical. A complete Dictionary of all pertaining to the Art of Cookery and Table Service. Edited by THEO. FRANCIS GARRETT, assisted by eminent Chefs de Cuisine and Confectioners. Profusely Illustrated with Coloured Plates and Engravings by HAROLD FURNESS, GEO. CRUIKSHANK, W. MUNN ANDREW, and others. *In 2 vols., large post 4to., cloth gilt, cushion edges, £3; carriage free, £3 1s. 6d.*

Cookery for Amateurs; or, French Dishes for English Homes of all Classes. Includes Simple Cookery, Middle-class Cookery, Superior Cookery, Cookery for Invalids, and Breakfast and Luncheon Cookery. By MADAME VALÉRIE. Second Edition. *In paper, price 1s., by post 1s. 2d.*

Cucumber Culture for Amateurs. Including also Melons, Vegetable Marrows, and Gourds. Illustrated. By W. J. MAY. *In paper, price 1s., by post 1s. 2d.*

Cyclist's Route Map of England and Wales. Shows clearly all the Main, and most of the Cross, Roads, Railroads, and the Distances between the Chief Towns, as well as the Mileage from London. In addition to this, Routes of *Thirty of the Most Interesting Tours* are printed in red. Fourth Edition, thoroughly revised. The map is printed on specially prepared vellum paper, and is the fullest, handiest, and best up-to-date tourist's map in the market. *In cloth, price* 1*s., by post* 1*s.* 2*d.*

Designing, Harmonic and Keyboard. Explaining a System whereby an endless Variety of Most Beautiful Designs suited to numberless Manufactures may be obtained by Unskilled Persons from any Printed Music. Illustrated by Numerous Explanatory Diagrams and Illustrative Examples. By C. H. WILKINSON. *Demy* 4*to, price* £2 2*s. nett.*

Dogs, Breaking and Training: Being Concise Directions for the proper education of Dogs, both for the Field and for Companions. Second Edition. By "PATHFINDER." With Chapters by HUGH DALZIEL. Illustrated. *In cloth gilt, price* 6*s.* 6*d., by post* 6*s.* 10*d.*

Dogs, British, Ancient and Modern: Their Varieties, History, and Characteristics. By HUGH DALZIEL, assisted by Eminent Fanciers. Beautifully Illustrated with COLOURED PLATES and full-page Engravings of Dogs of the Day, with numerous smaller illustrations in the text. This is the fullest work on the various breeds of dogs kept in England. In three volumes, *demy* 8*vo, cloth gilt, price* 10*s.* 6*d. each, by post* 11*s. each.*

Vol. I. Dogs Used in Field Sports.

Vol. II. Dogs Useful to Man in other Work than Field Sports; House and Toy Dogs.

Vol. III. Practical Kennel Management: A Complete Treatise on all Matters relating to the Proper Management of Dogs whether kept for the Show Bench, for the Field, or for Companions.

Dogs, Diseases of: Their Causes, Symptoms, and Treatment; Modes of Administering Medicines; Treatment in cases of Poisoning, &c. For the use of Amateurs. By HUGH DALZIEL. Fourth Edition. Entirely Re-written and brought up to Date. *In paper, price* 1*s., by post* 1*s.* 2*d.*; *in cloth gilt,* 2*s., by post* 2*s.* 3*d.*

Dog-Keeping, Popular: Being a Handy Guide to the General Management and Training of all Kinds of Dogs for Companions and Pets. By J. MAXTEE. Illustrated. *In paper, price* 1*s., by post* 1*s.* 2*d.*

Engravings and their Value. Containing a Dictionary of all the Greatest Engravers and their Works. By J. H. SLATER. New Edition, Revised and brought up to date, with latest Prices at Auction. *In cloth gilt, price* 15*s. nett, by post,* 15*s.* 5*d.*

Entertainments, Amateur, for Charitable and other Objects: How to Organise and Work them with Profit and Success. By ROBERT GANTHONY. *In coloured cover, price* 1*s., by post* 1*s.* 2*d.*

Fancy Work Series, Artistic. A Series of Illustrated Manuals on Artistic and Popular Fancy Work of various kinds. Each number is complete in itself, and issued at the uniform *price of* 6*d., by post* 7*d.* Now ready—(1) MACRAMÉ LACE (Second Edition); (2) PATCHWORK; (3) TATTING; (4) CREWEL WORK; (5) APPLIQUÉ; (6) FANCY NETTING.

Feathered Friends, Old and New. Being the Experience of many years' Observation of the Habits of British and Foreign Cage Birds. By DR. W. T. GREENE. Illustrated. *In cloth gilt, price* 5*s., by post* 5*s.* 4*d.*

Ferns, The Book of Choice: for the Garden, Conservatory, and Stove. Describing the best and most striking Ferns and Selaginellas, and giving explicit directions for their Cultivation, the formation of Rockeries, the arrangement of Ferneries, &c. By GEORGE SCHNEIDER. With numerous Coloured Plates and other Illustrations. *In* 3 *vols., large post* 4*to. Cloth gilt, price* £3 3*s. nett, by post* £3 5*s.*

Ferns, Choice British. Descriptive of the most beautiful Variations from the common forms, and their Culture. By C. T. DRUERY, F.L.S. Very accurate PLATES, and other Illustrations. *In cloth gilt, price* 2*s.* 6*d., by post* 2*s.* 9*d.*

Ferrets and Ferreting. Containing Instructions for the Breeding, Management, and Working of Ferrets. Second Edition, Re-written and greatly Enlarged. Illustrated. *In paper, price* 6*d., by post* 7*d.*

Fertility of Eggs Certificate. These are Forms of Guarantee given by the Sellers to the Buyers of Eggs for Hatching, undertaking to refund value of any unfertile eggs, or to replace them with good ones. Very valuable to sellers of eggs, as they induce purchases. *In books, with counterfoils, price* 6*d., by post* 7*d.*

Firework-Making for Amateurs. A complete, accurate, and easily-understood work on Making Simple and High-class Fireworks. By DR. W. H. BROWNE, M.A. *In coloured wrapper, price 2s 6d., by post 2s. 9d.*

Fisherman, The Practical. Dealing with the Natural History, the Legendary Lore, the Capture of British Fresh-Water Fish, and Tackle and Tackle-making. By J. H. KEENE. *In cloth gilt, price 7s. 6d., by post 7s. 10d.*

Fish Flesh, and Fowl When in Season, How to Select, Cook, and Serve. By MARY BARRETT BROWN. *In coloured wrapper, price 1s., by post 1s. 3d.*

Foreign Birds, Favourite, for Cages and Aviaries. How to Keep them in Health. Fully Illustrated. By W. T. GREENE, M.A., M.D., F.Z.S., &c. *In cloth, price 2s. 6d., by post 2s. 9d.*

Fox Terrier, The. Its History, Points, Breeding, Rearing, Preparing for Exhibition, and Coursing. By HUGH DALZIEL. Illustrated with Coloured Frontispiece and Plates. *In paper, price 1s., by post 1s. 2d.; cloth, 2s., by post 2s. 3d.*

Fox Terrier Stud Book. Edited by HUGH DALZIEL. *Price 3s. 6d. each, by post 3s. 9d. each.*

Vol. I., containing Pedigrees of over 1400 of the best-known Dogs, traced to their most remote known ancestors.
Vol. II. Pedigrees of 1544 Dogs, Show Record, &c.
Vol. III. Pedigrees of 1214 Dogs, Show Record, &c.
Vol. IV. Pedigrees of 1168 Dogs, Show Record, &c.
Vol. V. Pedigrees of 1662 Dogs, Show Record, &c.

Fretwork and Marquetry. A Practical Manual of Instructions in the Art of Fret-cutting and Marquetry Work. Profusely Illustrated. By D. DENNING. *In cloth, price 2s. 6d., by post 2s. 9d.*

Friesland Meres, A Cruise on the. By ERNEST R. SUFFLING. Illustrated. *In paper, price 1s., by post 1s. 2d.*

Fruit Culture for Amateurs. By S. T. WRIGHT. With Chapters on Insect and other Fruit Pests by W. D. DRURY. Illustrated. *In cloth gilt, price 3s. 6d., by post 3s. 9d.*

Game Preserving, Practical. Containing the fullest Directions for Rearing and Preserving both Winged and Ground Game, and Destroying Vermin; with other Information of Value to the Game Preserver. By W. CARNEGIE. Illustrated. *In cloth gilt, demy 8vo, price 21s., by post 21s. 5d.*

Games, the Book of a Hundred. By MARY WHITE. These Games are for Adults, and will be found extremely serviceable for Parlour Entertainment. They are Clearly Explained, are Ingenious, Clever, Amusing, and exceedingly Novel. *In stiff boards, price 2s. 6d. by post 2s. 9d.*

Gardening, Dictionary of. A Practical Encyclopædia of Horticulture, for Amateurs and Professionals. Illustrated with 2440 Engravings. Edited by G. NICHOLSON, Curator of the Royal Botanic Gardens, Kew; assisted by Prof. Trail, M.D., Rev. P. W. Myles, B.A., F.L.S., W. Watson, J. Garrett, and other Specialists. *In 4 vols., large post 4to. In cloth gilt, price £3, by post £3 2s.*

Gardening in Egypt. A Handbook of Gardening for Lower Egypt. With a Calendar of Work for the different Months of the Year. By WALTER DRAPER. *In cloth, price 3s. 6d., by post 3s. 9d.*

Goat, Book of the. Containing Full Particulars of the Various Breeds of Goats, and their Profitable Management. With many Plates. By H. STEPHEN HOLMES PEGLER. Third Edition, with Engravings and Coloured Frontispiece. *In cloth gilt, price 4s. 6d., by post 4s. 10d.*

Goat-Keeping for Amateurs: Being the Practical Management of Goats for Milking Purposes. Abridged from "The Book of the Goat." Illustrated. *In paper, price 1s., by post 1s. 2d.*

Grape Growing for Amateurs. A Thoroughly Practical Book on Successful Vine Culture. By E. MOLYNEUX. Illustrated. *In paper, price 1s., by post 1s. 2d.*

Greenhouse Management for Amateurs. The Best Greenhouses and Frames, and How to Build and Heat them, Illustrated Descriptions of the most suitable Plants, with general and Special Cultural Directions, and all necessary information for the Guidance of the Amateur. Second Edition, Revised and Enlarged. Magnificently Illustrated. By W. J. MAY. *In cloth gilt, price 5s., by post 5s. 4d.*

Greyhound, The: Its History, Points, Breeding, Rearing, Training, and Running. By HUGH DALZIEL. With Coloured Frontispiece. *In cloth gilt, demy 8vo., price 2s. 6d., by post 2s. 9d.*

Guinea Pig, The, for Food, Fur, and Fancy. Its Varieties and its Management. By C. CUMBERLAND, F.Z.S. Illustrated. *In coloured wrapper, price* 1s., *by post* 1s. 2d. *In cloth gilt, with coloured frontispiece, price* 2s. 6d., *by post* 2s. 9d.

Handwriting, Character Indicated by. With Illustrations in Support of the Theories advanced, taken from Autograph Letters of Statesmen, Lawyers, Soldiers, Ecclesiastics, Authors, Poets, Musicians, Actors, and other persons. Second Edition. By R. BAUGHAN. *In cloth gilt, price* 2s. 6d., *by post* 2s. 9d.

Hardy Perennials and Old-fashioned Garden Flowers. Descriptions, alphabetically arranged, of the most desirable Plants for Borders, Rockeries, and Shrubberies, including Foliage as well as Flowering Plants. By J. WOOD. Profusely Illustrated. *In cloth, price* 3s. 6d., *by post* 3s. 9d.

Hawk Moths, Book of British. A Popular and Practical Manual for all Lepidopterists. Copiously illustrated in black and white from the Author's own exquisite Drawings from Nature. By W. J. LUCAS, B.A. *In cloth, price* 3s. 6d., *by post* 3s. 9d.

Home Medicine and Surgery: A Dictionary of Diseases and Accidents, and their proper Home Treatment. For Family Use. By W. J. MACKENZIE, M.D. Illustrated. *In cloth, price* 2s. 6d., *by post* 2s. 9d.

Horse-Keeper, The Practical. By GEORGE FLEMING, C.B., LL.D., F.R.C.V.S., late Principal Veterinary Surgeon to the British Army, and Ex-President of the Royal College of Veterinary Surgeons. *In cloth, price* 3s. 6d., *by post* 3s. 10d.

Horse-Keeping for Amateurs. A Practical Manual on the Management of Horses, for the guidance of those who keep one or two for their personal use. By FOX RUSSELL. *In paper, price* 1s., *by post* 1s. 2d.; *cloth* 2s., *by post* 2s. 3d.

Horses, Diseases of: Their Causes, Symptoms, and Treatment. For the use of Amateurs. By HUGH DALZIEL. *In paper, price* 1s., *by post* 1s. 2d.; *cloth* 2s., *by post* 2s. 3d.

Incubators and their Management. By J. H. SUTCLIFFE. New Edition, Revised and Enlarged. Illustrated. *In paper, price* 1s., *by post* 1s. 2d.

Inland Watering Places. A Description of the Spas of Great Britain and Ireland, their Mineral Waters, and their Medicinal Value, and the attractions which they offer to Invalids and other Visitors. Profusely illustrated. A Companion Volume to "Seaside Watering Places." *In cloth, price* 2s. 6d., *by post* 2s. 10d.

Jack All Alone. Being a Collection of Descriptive Yachting Reminiscences. By FRANK COWPER, B.A., Author of "Sailing Tours." Illustrated. *In cloth gilt, price* 3s. 6d., *by post* 3s. 10d.

Journalism, Practical: How to Enter Thereon and Succeed. A book for all who think of "writing for the Press." By JOHN DAWSON. *In cloth gilt, price* 2s. 6d., *by post* 2s. 9d.

Laying Hens, How to Keep and to Rear Chickens in Large or Small Numbers, in Absolute Confinement, with Perfect Success. By MAJOR G. F. MORANT. *In paper, price* 6d., *by post* 7d.

Library Manual, The. A Guide to the Formation of a Library, and the Values of Rare and Standard Books. By J. H. SLATER, Barrister-at-Law. Third Edition. Revised and Greatly Enlarged. *In cloth gilt, price* 7s. 6d. *nett, by post* 7s. 10d.

Magic Lanterns, Modern. A Guide to the Management of the Optical Lantern, for the Use of Entertainers, Lecturers, Photograpers, Teachers, and others. By R. CHILD BAYLEY. *In paper, price* 1s., *by post* 1s. 2d.

Mice, Fancy: Their Varieties, Management, and Breeding. Third Edition, with additional matter and Illustrations. *In coloured wrapper representing different varieties, price* 1s., *by post* 1s. 2d.

Millinery, Handbook of. A Practical Manual of Instruction for Ladies. Illustrated. By MME. ROSÉE, Court Milliner, Principal of the School of Millinery. *In paper, price* 1s., *by post* 1s. 2d.

Model Yachts and Boats: Their Designing, Making, and Sailing. Illustrated with 118 Designs and Working Diagrams. By J. DU V. GROSVENOR. *In leatherette, price* 5s., *by post* 5s. 3d.

Monkeys, Pet, and How to Manage Them. Illustrated. By ARTHUR PATTERSON. *In cloth gilt, price* 2s. 6d., *by post* 2s. 9d.

Mountaineering, Welsh. A Complete and Handy Guide to all the Best Roads and Bye-Paths by which the Tourist should Ascend the Welsh Mountains. By A. W. PERRY. With numerous Maps. *In cloth gilt, price 2s. 6d., by post 2s. 9d.*

Mushroom Culture for Amateurs. With Full Directions for Successful Growth in Houses, Sheds, Cellars, and Pots, on Shelves, and Out of Doors. Illustrated. By W. J. MAY. *In paper, price 1s., by post 1s. 2d.*

Natural History Sketches among the Carnivora—Wild and Domesticated; with Observations on their Habits and Mental Faculties. By ARTHUR NICOLS, F.G.S., F.R.G.S. Illustrated. *In cloth gilt, price 2s. 6d., by post 2s. 9d.*

Naturalist's Directory, The, for 1896 (fourth year of issue). Invaluable to all Students and Collectors. *In paper, price 1s., by post 1s. 1d.*

Needlework, Dictionary of. An Encyclopædia of Artistic, Plain, and Fancy Needlework; Plain, practical, complete, and magnificently Illustrated. By S. F. A. CAULFEILD and B. C. SAWARD. *In demy 4to, 528pp, 829 Illustrations, extra cloth gilt, plain edges, cushioned bevelled boards, price 21s. nett, by post 21s. 9d.; with COLOURED PLATES, elegant satin brocade cloth binding, and coloured edges, 31s. 6d. nett, by post 32s.*

Orchids: Their Culture and Management, with Descriptions of all the Kinds in General Cultivation. Illustrated by Coloured Plates and Engravings. By W. WATSON, Assistant-Curator, Royal Botanic Gardens, Kew; Assisted by W. BEAN, Foreman, Royal Gardens, Kew. Second Edition, Revised and with Extra Plates *In cloth gilt and gilt edges, price £1 1s. nett, by post £1 1s. 6d.*

Painters and Their Works. A Work of the Greatest Value to Collectors and such as are interested in the Art, as it gives, besides Biographical Sketches of all the Artists of Repute (not now living) from the 13th Century to the present date, the Market Value of the Principal Works Painted by Them, with Full Descriptions of Same. *In 3 vols., cloth, price 15s. nett per vol., by post 15s. 5d., or 37s. 6d. nett the set of 3, by post 38s. 3d.*

Painting, Decorative. A practical Handbook on Painting and Etching upon Textiles, Pottery, Porcelain, Paper, Vellum, Leather, Glass, Wood, Stone, Metals, and Plaster, for the Decoration of our Homes. By B. C. SAWARD. *In cloth gilt, price 3s. 6d., by post 3s. 9d.*

Parcel Post Dispatch Book (registered). An invaluable book for all who send parcels by post. Provides Address Labels, Certificate of Posting, and Record of Parcels Dispatched. By the use of this book parcels are insured against loss or damage to the extent of £2. Authorised by the Post Office. *Price 1s., by post 1s. 2d., for 100 parcels; larger sizes if required.*

Parrakeets, Popular. How to Keep and Breed Them. By DR. W. T. GREENE, M.D., M.A., F.Z.S., &c. *Price 1s., by post, 1s. 2d.*

Parrot, The Grey, and How to Treat it. By W. T. GREENE, M.D., M.A., F.Z.S., &c. *Price 1s., by post 1s. 2d.*

Parrots, the Speaking. The Art of Keeping and Breeding the principal Talking Parrots in Confinement. By DR. KARL RUSS. Illustrated with COLOURED PLATES and Engravings. *In cloth gilt, price 5s., by post 5s. 4d.*

Patience, Games of, for one or more Players. How to Play 142 different Games of Patience. By M. WHITMORE JONES. Illustrated. Series I., 39 games; Series II., 34 games; Series III., 33 games; Series IV., 37 games. Each 1s., *by post 1s. 2d. The four bound together in cloth gilt, price 5s., by post 5s. 4d.*

Perspective, The Essentials of. With numerous Illustrations drawn by the Author. By L. W. MILLER, Principal of the School of Industrial Art of the Pennsylvania Museum, Philadelphia. *Price 6s. 6d., by post 6s. 10d.*

Pheasant-Keeping for Amateurs. A Practical Handbook on the Breeding, Rearing, and General Management of Fancy Pheasants in Confinement By GEO. HORNE. Fully Illustrated. *In cloth gilt, price 3s. 6d., by post 3s. 9d.*

Photographic Printing Processes, Popular. A Practical Guide to Printing with Gelatino-Chloride, Artigue, Platinotype, Carbon, Bromide, Collodio-Chloride, Bichromated Gum, and other Sensitised Papers. Illustrated. By H. MACLEAN, F.R.P.S. *Price 2s. 6d., by post 2s. 10d.*

Photography (Modern) for Amateurs. New and Revised Edition. By J. EATON FEARN. *In paper, price 1s., by post 1s. 2d.*

Pianofortes, Tuning and Repairing. The Amateur's Guide to the Practical Management of a Piano without the intervention of a Professional. By CHARLES BABBINGTON *In paper, price 6d., by post 6½d.*

Picture-Frame Making for Amateurs. Being Practical Instructions in the Making of various kinds of Frames for Paintings, Drawings, Photographs, and Engravings. Illustrated. By the REV. J. LUKIN. *In paper, price* 1s., *by post* 1s 2d.

Pig, Book of the. The Selection, Breeding, Feeding, and Management of the Pig; the Treatment of its Diseases; the Curing and Preserving of Hams, Bacon, and other Pork Foods; and other information appertaining to Pork Farming. By PROFESSOR JAMES LONG. Fully Illustrated with Portraits of Prize Pigs, Plans of Model Piggeries, &c. *In cloth gilt, price* 10s. 6d., *by post* 10s. 11d.

Pig-Keeping, Practical: A Manual for Amateurs, based on personal Experience in Breeding, Feeding, and Fattening; also in Buying and Selling Pigs at Market Prices. By R. D. GARRATT. *In paper, price* 1s., *by post* 1s. 2d.

Pigeons, Fancy. Containing full Directions for the Breeding and Management of Fancy Pigeons, and Descriptions of every known Variety, together with all other information of interest or use to Pigeon Fanciers. Third Edition. 18 COLOURED PLATES, and 22 other full-page Illustrations. By J. C. LYELL. *In cloth gilt, price* 10s. 6d., *by post* 10s. 10d.

Pigeon-Keeping for Amateurs. A Complete Guide to the Amateur Breeder of Domestic and Fancy Pigeons. By J. C. LYELL. Illustrated. *In cloth, price* 2s. 6d., *by post* 2s. 9d.

Polishes and Stains for Wood: A Complete Guide to Polishing Woodwork, with Directions for Staining, and Full Information for Making the Stains, Polishes, &c., in the simplest and most satisfactory manner. By DAVID DENNING. *In paper*, 1s., *by post* 1s. 2d.

Pool, Games of. Describing Various English and American Pool Games, and giving the Rules in full. Illustrated *In paper, price* 1s., *by post* 1s. 2d.

Postage Stamps, and their Collection. A Practical Handbook for Collectors of Postal Stamps, Envelopes, Wrappers, and Cards. By OLIVER FIRTH, Member of the Philatelic Societies of London, Leeds, and Bradford. Profusely Illustrated. *In cloth gilt, price* 3s. 6d., *by post* 3s. 10d.

Postage Stamps of Europe, The Adhesive: A Practical Guide to their Collection, Identification, and Classification. Especially designed for the use of those commencing the Study. By W. A. S. WESTOBY. Beautifully Illustrated. *In Parts*, 1s. *each, by post* 1s. 2d.

Postmarks, History of British. With 350 Illustrations and a List of Numbers used in Obliterations. By J. H. DANIELS. *In cloth, price* 2s. 6d., *by post* 2s. 9d.

Pottery and Porcelain, English. A Guide for Collectors. Handsomely Illustrated with Engravings of Specimen Pieces and the Marks used by the different Makers. New Edition, Revised and Enlarged. By the REV. E. A. DOWNMAN. *In cloth gilt, price* 5s., *by post* 5s. 3d.

Poultry-Farming, Profitable. Describing in Detail the Methods that Give the Best Results, and pointing out the Mistakes to be Avoided. Illustrated. By J. H. SUTCLIFFE. *Price* 1s., *by post* 1s. 2d.

Poultry-Keeping, Popular. A Practical and Complete Guide to Breeding and Keeping Poultry for Eggs or for the Table. By F. A. MACKENZIE. Illustrated. *In paper, price* 1s., *by post* 1s. 2d.

Poultry and Pigeon Diseases Their Causes, Symptoms, and Treatment. A Practical Manual for all Fanciers. By QUINTIN CRAIG and JAMES LYELL. *In paper, price* 1s., *by post* 1s. 2d.

Poultry for Prizes and Profit. Contains: Breeding Poultry for Prizes, Exhibition Poultry and Management of the Poultry Yard. Handsomely Illustrated. Second Edition. By PROF. JAMES LONG. *In cloth gilt, price* 2s. 6d., *by post* 2s. 10d.

Rabbit, Book of The. A Complete Work on Breeding and Rearing all Varieties of Fancy Rabbits, giving their History, Variations, Uses, Points, Selection, Mating, Management, &c., &c. SECOND EDITION. Edited by KEMPSTER W. KNIGHT. Illustrated with Coloured and other Plates. *In cloth gilt, price* 10s. 6d., *by post* 10s. 11d.

Rabbits, Diseases of: Their Causes, Symptoms, and Cure. With a Chapter on THE DISEASES OF CAVIES. Reprinted from "The Book of the Rabbit" and "The Guinea Pig for Food, Fur Fancy." *In paper, price* 1s., *by post* 1s. 2d.

Rabbits for Prizes and Profit. The Proper Management of Fancy Rabbits in Health and Disease, for Pets or the Market, and Descriptions of every known Variety, with Instructions for Breeding Good Specimens. Illustrated. By CHARLES RAYSON. *In cloth gilt, price 2s. 6d., by post 2s. 9d.* Also in Sections, as follows:

General Management of Rabbits. Including Hutches, Breeding, Feeding, Diseases and their Treatment, Rabbit Courts, &c. Fully Illustrated. *In paper, price 1s., by post 1s. 2d.*

Exhibition Rabbits. Being descriptions of all Varieties of Fancy Rabbits, their Points of Excellence, and how to obtain them. Illustrated. *In paper, price 1s., by post 1s. 2d.*

Road Charts (Registered). For Army Men, Volunteers, Cyclists, and other Road Users. By S. W. H. DIXON and A. B. H. CLERKE. No. 1.—London to Brighton. *Price 2d., by post 2½d.*

Roses for Amateurs. A Practical Guide to the Selection and Cultivation of the best Roses. Illustrated. By the REV. J. HONYWOOD D'OMBRAIN, Hon. Sec. Nat. Rose Soc. *In paper, price 1s., by post 1s. 2d.*

Sailing Guide to the Solent and Poole Harbour, with Practical Hints as to Living and Cooking on, and Working a Small Yacht. By LIEUT.-COL. T. G. CUTHELL. Illustrated with Coloured Charts. *In cloth gilt, price 2s. 6d., by post 2s. 9d.*

Sailing Tours. The Yachtman's Guide to the Cruising Waters of the English and Adjacent Coasts. With Descriptions of every Creek, Harbour, and Roadstead on the Course. With numerous Charts printed in Colours, showing Deep water, Shoals, and Sands exposed at low water, with sounding. *In Crown 8vo., cloth gilt.* By FRANK COWPER, B.A.

Vol. I., the Coasts of Essex and Suffolk, from the Thames to Aldborough. Six Charts. *Price 5s., by post 5s. 3d.*

Vol. II. The South Coast, from the Thames to the Scilly Islands, twenty-five Charts. *Price 7s. 6d., by post 7s. 10d.*

Vol. III. The Coast of Brittany, from L'Abervrach to St. Nazaire, and an Account of the Loire. Twelve Charts. *Price 7s. 6d., by post 7s. 10d.*

Vol. IV. The West Coast, from Land's End to Mull of Galloway, including the East Coast of Ireland. Thirty Charts. *Price 10s. 6d., by post 10s. 10d.*

Vol. V. The Coasts of Scotland and the N.E. of England down to Aldborough. Forty Charts. *Price 10s. 6d., by post 10s. 10d.*

St. Bernard, The. Its History, Points, Breeding, and Rearing. By HUGH DALZIEL. Illustrated with Coloured Frontispiece and Plates. *In cloth, price 2s 6d., by post 2s. 9d.*

St. Bernard Stud Book. Edited by HUGH DALZIEL. *Price 3s. 6d. each, by post 3s. 9d. each.*

Vol. I. Pedigrees of 1278 of the best known Dogs traced to their most remote known ancestors, Show Record, &c.

Vol. II. Pedigrees of 564 Dogs, Show Record, &c.

Sea-Fishing for Amateurs. Practical Instructions to Visitors at Seaside Places for Catching Sea-Fish from Pier-heads, Shore, or Boats, principally by means of Hand Lines, with a very useful List of Fishing Stations, the Fish to be caught there, and the Best Seasons. By FRANK HUDSON. Illustrated. *In paper, price 1s., by post 1s. 2d.*

Sea-Fishing on the English Coast. The Art of Making and Using Sea-Tackle, with a full account of the methods in vogue during each month of the year, and a Detailed Guide for Sea-Fishermen to all the most Popular Watering Places on the English Coast. By F. G. AFLALO. Illustrated. *In cloth gilt, price 2s. 6d., by post 2s. 9d.*

Sea-Life, Realities of. Describing the Duties, Prospects, and Pleasures of a Young Sailor in the Mercantile Marine. By H. E. ACRAMAN COATE. With a Preface by J. R. DIGGLE, M.A., M.L.S.B. *In cloth, price 3s. 6d., by post 3s. 10d.*

Seaside Watering Places. A Description of the Holiday Resorts on the Coasts of England and Wales, the Channel Islands, and the Isle of Man, giving full particulars of them and their attractions, and all information likely to assist persons in selecting places in which to spend their Holidays according to their individual tastes. Illustrated. Eighth Edition. *In cloth, price 2s. 6d., by post 2s. 10d.*

Sea Terms, a Dictionary of. For the use of Yachtsmen, Amateur Boatmen, and Beginners. By A. ANSTED. Fully Illustrated. *Cloth gilt, price 7s. 6d. nett, by post 7s. 11d.*

Shadow Entertainments, and How to Work them: being Something about Shadows, and the way to make them Profitable and Funny. By A. PATTERSON. *In paper, price 1s., by post 1s. 2d.*

Shave, An Easy: The Mysteries, Secrets, and Whole Art of, laid bare for 1s., *by post 1s. 2d.* Edited by JOSEPH MORTON.

Sheet Metal, Working in: Being Practical Instructions for Making and Mending Small Articles in Tin, Copper, Iron, Zinc, and Brass. Illustrated. Third Edition. By the Rev. J. LUKIN, B.A. *In paper, price 1s., by post 1s. 1d.*

Shorthand, on Gurney's System (Improved), LESSONS IN: Being Instructions in the Art of Shorthand Writing as used in the Service of the two Houses of Parliament. By R. E. MILLER. *In paper, price 1s., by post 1s. 2d.*

Shorthand, Exercises in, for Daily Half Hours, on a Newly-devised and Simple Method, free from the Labour of Learning. Illustrated. Being Part II. of "Lessons in Shorthand on Gurney's System (Improved)." By R. E. MILLER. *In paper, price 9d., by post 10d.*

Skating Cards: An Easy Method of Learning Figure Skating, as the Cards *can be used on the Ice. In cloth case, 2s. 6d., by post 2s. 9d.; leather, 3s. 6d., by post 3s. 9d.* A cheap form is issued printed on paper and made up as a small book, 1s., *by post 1s. 1d.*

Sleight of Hand. A Practical Manual of Legerdemain for Amateurs and Others. New Edition, Revised and Enlarged Profusely Illustrated. By E. SACHS. *In cloth gilt, price 6s. 6d., by post 6s. 10d.*

Snakes, Marsupials, and Birds. A Charming Book of Anecdotes, Adventures, and Zoological Notes. A capital Book for Boys. By ARTHUR NICOLS, F.G.S., F.R.G.S., &c. Illustrated. *In cloth gilt, price 3s. 6d., by post 3s. 10d.*

Taxidermy, Practical. A Manual of Instruction to the Amateur in Collecting, Preserving, and Setting-up Natural History Specimens of all kinds. With Examples and Working Diagrams. By MONTAGU BROWNE, F.Z.S., Curator of Leicester Museum. Second Edition. *In cloth gilt, price 7s. 6d., by post 7s. 10d.*

Thames Guide Book. From Lechlade to Richmond. For Boating Men, Anglers, Picnic Parties, and all Pleasure-seekers on the River. Arranged on an entirely new plan. Second Edition, profusely Illustrated. *In cloth, price 1s. 6d., by post 1s. 9d.*

Tomato and Fruit Growing as an Industry for Women. Lectures given at the Forestry Exhibition, Earl's Court, during July and August, 1893. By GRACE HARRIMAN, Practical Fruit Grower and County Council Lecturer. *In paper, price 1s., by post 1s. 1d.*

Tomato Culture for Amateurs. A Practical and very Complete Manual on the subject. By B. C. RAVENSCROFT. Illustrated. *In paper, price 1s., by post 1s. 1d.*

Trapping, Practical: Being some Papers on Traps and Trapping for Vermin, with a Chapter on General Bird Trapping and Snaring. By W. CARNEGIE. *In paper, price 1s., by post 1s. 2d.*

Turning for Amateurs: Being Descriptions of the Lathe and its Attachments and Tools, with Minute Instructions for their Effective Use on Wood, Metal, Ivory, and other Materials. Second Edition, Revised and Enlarged. By JAMES LUKIN, B.A. Illustrated with 144 Engravings. *In cloth gilt, price 2s. 6d., by post 2s. 9d.*

Turning Lathes. A Manual for Technical Schools and Apprentices. A Guide to Turning, Screw-cutting, Metal-spinning, &c. Edited by JAMES LUKIN, B.A. Third Edition. With 194 Illustrations. *In cloth gilt, price 3s., by post 3s. 3d.*

Vamp, How to. A Practical Guide to the Accompaniment of Songs by the Unskilled Musician. With Examples. *In paper, price 9d, by post 10d.*

Vegetable Culture for Amateurs. Containing Concise Directions for the Cultivation of Vegetables in Small Gardens so as to insure Good Crops. With Lists of the Best Varieties of each Sort. By W. J. MAY. Illustrated. *In paper, price 1s., by post 1s. 2d.*

Ventriloquism, Practical. A thoroughly reliable Guide to the Art of Voice Throwing and Vocal Mimicry, Vocal Instrumentation, Ventriloquial Figures, Entertaining, &c. By ROBERT GANTHONY. Numerous Illustrations. *In cloth gilt, price* 2*s.* 6*d., by post* 2*s.* 9*d.*

Violins (Old) and their Makers: Including some References to those of Modern Times. By JAMES M. FLEMING. Illustrated with Facsimiles of Tickets, Sound-Holes, &c. *In cloth gilt, price* 6*s.* 6*d. nett, by post* 6*s.* 10*d.*

Violin School, Practical, for Home Students. Instructions and Exercises in Violin Playing, for the use of Amateurs, Self-learners, Teachers, and others. With a Supplement on "Easy Legato Studies for the Violin." By J. M. FLEMING. *Demy* 4*to, cloth gilt, price* 9*s.* 6*d., by post* 10*s.* 2*d.* Without Supplement, *price* 7*s.* 6*d., by post* 8*s.*

Vivarium, The. Being a Full Description of the most Interesting Snakes, Lizards, and other Reptiles, and How to Keep Them Satisfactorily in Confinement. By REV. G. C. BATEMAN. Beautifully Illustrated. *In cloth gilt, price* 7*s.* 6*d. nett, by post* 8*s.*

War Medals and Decorations. A Manual for Collectors, with some account of Civil Rewards for Valour. Beautifully Illustrated. By D. HASTINGS IRWIN. *In cloth gilt, price* 7*s.* 6*d., by post* 7*s.* 10*d.*

Whippet and Race-Dog, The: How to Breed, Rear, Train, Race, and Exhibit the Whippet, the Management of Race Meetings, and Original Plans of Courses. By FREEMAN LLOYD. *In cloth gilt, price* 3*s.* 6*d., by post* 3*s.* 10*d.*

Whist, Modern Scientific. A Practical Manual on new Lines, and with Illustrative Hands. Printed in Colour. By C. J. MELROSE. *In cloth gilt, price* 6*s., by post* 6*s.* 6*d.*

Wildfowling, Practical: A Book on Wildfowl and Wildfowl Shooting. By HY. SHARP. The result of 25 years' experience in Wildfowl Shooting under all sorts of conditions of locality as well as circumstances. Profusely Illustrated. *Demy* 8*vo, cloth gilt, price* 12*s.* 6*d. nett, by post* 12*s.* 10*d.*

Wild Sports in Ireland. Being Picturesque and Entertaining Descriptions of several visits paid to Ireland, with Practical Hints likely to be of service to the Angler, Wildfowler, and Yachtsman. By JOHN BICKERDYKE, Author of "The Book of the All-Round Angler," &c. Beautifully Illustrated from Photographs taken by the Author. *In cloth gilt, price* 6*s., by post* 6*s.* 4*d.*

Window Ticket Writing. Containing full Instructions on the Method of Mixing and Using the Various Inks, &c., required, Hints on Stencilling as applied to Ticket Writing, together with Lessons on Glass Writing, Japanning on Tin, &c. Especially written for the use of Learners and Shop Assistants. By WM. C. SCOTT. *In paper, price* 1*s., by post* 1*s.* 2*d.*

Wire and Sheet Gauges of the World. Compared and Compiled by C. A. B. PFEILSCHMIDT, of Sheffield. *In paper, price* 1*s., by post* 1*s.* 1*d.*

Wood Carving for Amateurs. Full Instructions for producing all the different varieties of Carvings. SECOND EDITION. Edited by D. DENNING. *In paper, price* 1*s., by post* 1*s.* 2*d.*

FICTION LIBRARY.

Decameron of a Hypnotist. Tales of Dread. By E. SUFFLING, Author of "The Story Hunter," &c. With Illustrations. *Cloth gilt,* 3*s.* 6*d., by post* 3*s.* 10*d.*

www.ingramcontent.com/pod-product-compliance
Lightning Source LLC
Chambersburg PA
CBHW030537270326
41927CB00008B/1416
9783742862907